Hans G. Hoffmann

Englische Sprachgebrauchsübungen

Wiederholung von Grammatik
und Idiomatik
Ein systematisches Arbeitsbuch

Max Hueber Verlag

Hans G. Hoffmann
ENGLISCHE SPRACHGEBRAUCHSÜBUNGEN
Wiederholung von Grammatik und Idiomatik
Ein systematisches Arbeitsbuch

Sprachliche Beratung: Juliet Averay, Alan C. Phillips, Michael Presswood
Verlagsredaktion: Gernot Häublein
Umschlagentwurf und Layout: Karl Schaumann

Redaktionsschluß der 1. Auflage: Februar 1974

ISBN 3-19-00.2178-3
© 1974 Max Hueber Verlag München
4 3   1980   79   78
Die jeweils letzten Ziffern bezeichnen Zahl und Jahr des Druckes.
Alle Drucke dieser Auflage können nebeneinander benutzt werden.
Satz: Gebr. Parcus, München
Druck: Ludwig Auer, Donauwörth
Printed in Germany

VORWORT

In diesem Arbeitsbuch werden die Hauptprobleme des englischen Sprachgebrauchs in 60 Kapiteln systematisch geübt. Es handelt sich um "übergreifende", lehrbuchunabhängige Grammatik- und Wortschatzübungen, die besonders für die Aufarbeitung von Lücken und die Vorbereitung auf Prüfungen (wie etwa VHS-Zertifikat oder Abitur) geeignet sind. Um mit diesem Buch erfolgreich arbeiten zu können, sollte der Lernende Vorkenntnisse von mindestens zwei Jahren haben.

Die nach jeder Kapitelüberschrift in Klammern gesetzten Zahlen verweisen auf die Seiten der *Englischen Mindestgrammatik* des gleichen Verfassers (Hueber-Nr. 2155), auf denen grammatische Erläuterungen zu dem betreffenden Sprachgebrauchsproblem zu finden sind. Die Hinzunahme der *Englischen Mindestgrammatik* ist also nützlich, aber nicht unbedingt erforderlich.

Dieses Buch ist vor allem für die unterrichtsbegleitende Eigenarbeit der Englischlernenden gedacht. Aus diesem Grund ist den Übungen ein vollständiger Lösungsschlüssel beigegeben (S. 67ff.). Bei Aufgaben mit mehr als einer richtigen Lösung werden häufig vorkommende Alternativkonstruktionen nach einem Schrägstrich (/) aufgeführt.

Der Lösungsschlüssel hätte an Übersichtlichkeit verloren, wenn der Verfasser in Fällen wie *has not* / *hasn't* jeweils beide Formen angegeben hätte. Hier soll der allgemeine Hinweis genügen, daß in der Regel neben der ungekürzten Form auch die Kurzform und umgekehrt statt der Kurzform die ungekürzte Form stehen kann. Die Wahl der einen oder anderen Form hängt von der Kommunikationssituation und den Intentionen des Sprechers oder Schreibers ab. Zusätzlich zu den in der *Englischen Mindestgrammatik* (S. 144–145) gegebenen Hinweisen seien hier noch tabellarisch einige Kriterien für den Gebrauch der beiden Formen genannt:

Ungekürzte Form (Beispiel: *is not*)	Kurzform (Beispiel: *isn't*)
feierlich-langsam gesprochen	normal-umgangssprachlich gesprochen
mit heraushebender Betonung	ohne heraushebende Betonung
formeller Schrifttext	betont umgangssprachlicher Schrifttext
förmlicher Briefstil	familiärer Briefstil

Am Ende der meisten Übungskapitel finden sich englisch-deutsche Vokabel-
hinweise, die dem Lernenden das Bearbeiten der Übungen erleichtern
sollen. Die ausführlichen Wortschatzregister (Englisch S. 83 ff., Deutsch
S. 89 ff.) ermöglichen ein schnelles Auffinden der in den Vokabelhinweisen
behandelten Wörter.

Das Grammatikregister (S. 95 ff.) bietet zusätzlich zum Inhaltsverzeichnis
eine Orientierungshilfe beim Aufsuchen bestimmter Grammatikkapitel.

Zur Beachtung

Die in Klammern gesetzten **Zahlen** in den Kapitelüberschriften verweisen auf die Seiten der *Englischen Mindestgrammatik* von Hans G.
Hoffmann (Hueber-Nr. 2155), auf denen grammatische Erläuterungen
zu dem betreffenden Sprachgebrauchsproblem zu finden sind.

Im Schlüssel (S. 67 ff.) trennt ein **Schrägstrich** (/) jeweils gleichwertige
Alternativlösungen

Der Zusatz **U.S.** bezeichnet im Schlüssel Alternativkonstruktionen, die
vor allem im amerikanischen Sprachgebrauch üblich sind.

INHALTSVERZEICHNIS

Supply the plural form of the noun in brackets.

a. These ...... are not used for long-distance flights. (aircraft)
b. The ...... are still at school. (child)
c. He caught five ...... in all – one for each member of the family. (fish)
d. His ...... were aching after the dance. (foot)
e. The ...... on the big tree in the garden are turning yellow. (leaf)
f. I'm sure there are ...... in the cellar. (mouse)
g. I paid fifty ...... for this pen. (penny)
h. There were two ...... standing at the corner. (policeman)
i. The best way to keep the grass short is to put some ...... on it. (sheep)
j. You ought to brush your ...... after each meal. (tooth)

long-distance flight [flait]	Langstreckenflug
catch – caught [kɔ:t] – caught	fangen – fing – gefangen
we have nine tickets in all	wir haben insgesamt neun Karten
his back ached [eikt]	ihm tat der Rücken weh
she turned pale [tə:nd]	sie wurde bleich
at the corner ['kɔːnə]	an der Ecke
keep the grass short [grɑ:s]	das Gras kurz halten
she brushed her hair [brʌʃt]	sie bürstete sich die Haare

Please translate.

a. Seine Ratschläge wurden nicht befolgt. *weren't followed*
b. Der Inhalt der Kisten wurde nicht beschädigt. *wasn't damaged*
c. Die Möbel werden morgen geliefert.
d. Deine Brille ist auf dem Tisch im Wohnzimmer.
e. Die Ware ist gerade angekommen.
f. Hier sind einige wichtige Informationen.
g. Seine Französischkenntnisse sind begrenzt.
h. Es sind beträchtliche Fortschritte gemacht worden. *have been achieved / not made*
i. Die Treppe ist für den Hund zu steil.
j. Diese Hose war ziemlich teuer.

advice [əd'vais]	Ratschlag
contents ['kɔntents]	Inhalt
case [keis]	Kiste
deliver something to somebody	jemandem etwas liefern
living room ['liviŋ rum]	Wohnzimmer
important [im'pɔ:tənt]	wichtig
his knowledge is very limited	sein Wissen ist sehr begrenzt
he has considerable debts [dets]	er hat beträchtliche Schulden
a steep hill [sti:p]	ein steiler Berg
the dress was rather expensive	das Kleid war ziemlich teuer

Choose the correct verb form.

a. Ten dollars (is, are) a lot of money for a little boy.
b. There (is, are) about 500 gallons of oil left in the tank.
c. It (is, are) always the children who suffer most in such a situation.
d. The news (was, were) not very encouraging.
e. The Netherlands (has, have) an estimated 70 days' reserve of oil.
f. The people (is, are) fed up with the endless price increases.
g. The police (was, were) praised for handling the case so successfully.
h. The United States (faces, face) a serious energy crisis.

gallon ['gælən]	(*brit.*: = 4,55 Liter;
	U.S.: = 3,78 Liter)
there's nothing left ['nʌθiŋ]	es ist nichts übrig
suffer from a disease [di'zi:z]	an einer Krankheit leiden
encourage somebody [in'kʌridʒ]	jemanden ermutigen
estimate the cost [kɔst]	die Kosten schätzen
I'm fed up with your nagging	ich habe dein Nörgeln satt
price increase ['inkri:s]	Preiserhöhung
praise somebody [preiz]	jemanden loben
handle a case [keis]	einen Fall abwickeln
face a crisis ['kraisis]	vor einer Krise stehen

4 | Mit oder ohne the? (18–23)

Supply *the* where necessary.

a. There's a large new supermarket in ...... High Street.
b. He says that ...... life is pleasant in ...... Switzerland.
c. Can ...... modern man live without ...... electricity?
d. ...... Mount Everest is much higher than ...... Mont Blanc or ...... Matterhorn.
e. I used to play ...... piano quite well, but now I'm completely out of ...... practice.
f. A politician can't afford to ignore ...... public opinion.
g. We hardly ever listen to ...... radio, but we often watch ...... television.
h. There was a huge demonstration in ...... Trafalgar Square yesterday.
i. Don't ...... most housewives go to ...... town by ...... bus?
j. The poorest people usually have ...... most children.

a pleasant life ['pleznt]	ein angenehmes Leben
electricity [ilek'trisiti]	Elektrizität; (elektr.) Strom
I used to live here ['juːs tə]	ich habe früher hier gewohnt
piano ['pjænəu]	Klavier
politician [pɔli'tiʃn]	Politiker
I can't afford to stay at a hotel	ich kann mir nicht leisten, in einem Hotel zu wohnen
he ignored my advice [ig'nɔːd]	er ignorierte meinen Rat
a huge demonstration [hjuːdʒ]	eine gewaltige Demonstration
housewife ['hauswaif]	Hausfrau
he usually gets up at six ['juːʒuəli]	meistens steht er um sechs auf

Please translate.

a. Er ist immer in Eile.
b. Er raucht zwanzig Zigaretten pro Tag.
c. Ich habe eine wichtige Information für Sie.
d. Welche Farbe wäre Ihnen am liebsten?
e. Wir verkaufen tausend Flaschen im Monat.
f. Als Engländerin weiß sie, wie man guten Tee macht.
g. Was für ein herrliches Wetter wir doch haben!
h. Warum liest du zur Abwechslung nicht mal was?
i. Wenn du Fieber hast, bleibst du besser im Bett.
j. Mein Schwager, der Rechtsanwalt ist, hat mir einen guten Rat gegeben.

he only smokes cigarettes [sigə'rets]	er raucht nur Zigaretten
it's very important [im'pɔ:tənt]	es ist sehr wichtig
information [infə'meiʃn]	Information(en); Auskunft; Auskünfte
red is my favourite colour ['feivərit 'kʌlə]	rot ist meine Lieblingsfarbe
a bottle of whisky ['bɔtl]	eine Flasche Whisky
Englishwoman ['iŋgliʃwumən]	Engländerin
wonderful weather ['weðə]	herrliches Wetter
you need a change [tʃeinʒ]	du brauchst Abwechslung
stay in bed [bed]	im Bett bleiben
brother-in-law ['brʌðər in lɔ:]	Schwager
lawyer ['lɔ:jə]	Rechtsanwalt

Please translate.

a. Seine Tochter ist genauso unangenehm wie er.
b. Es ist nicht so einfach, wie du vielleicht denkst.
c. Der Bahnhof ist sogar noch weiter weg als der Flughafen.
d. Sein ältester Sohn ist zwei Jahre älter als ich.
e. Der Patient wird immer unruhiger.
f. Je ruhiger das Hotel ist, desto besser.
g. Er war mehr tot als lebendig, als er ankam.
h. Dieser Wolkenkratzer ist eines der höchsten Gebäude der Welt.
i. Er ist einer der intelligentesten Menschen, die ich kenne.
j. Du kannst die Rechnung bezahlen. Du hast das meiste Geld.
k. Die neuesten Nachrichten sind nicht sehr ermutigend.
l. Welches ist der nächste Weg zum Rathaus?

unpleasant [ʌnˈpleznt]	unangenehm
a simple task [tɑːsk]	eine einfache Aufgabe
airport [ˈɛəpɔːt]	Flughafen
he was getting restless [ˈrestlis]	er wurde unruhig
a quiet room [ˈkwaiət]	ein ruhiges Zimmer
he was buried alive [ˈberid]	er wurde lebendig begraben
skyscraper [ˈskaiskreipə]	Wolkenkratzer
a tall building [ˈbildiŋ]	ein hohes Gebäude
pay a bill [pei]	eine Rechnung bezahlen
encourage somebody [inˈkʌridʒ]	jemanden ermutigen
town hall [ˈtaun ˈhɔːl]	Rathaus

Please translate.

a. Das Schlimmste sollte noch kommen.
b. Er ist der Beste in der Gruppe.
c. Wer wird sich um die Kranken kümmern?
d. Kinder und Kranke wurden zuerst evakuiert.
e. Die Engländer haben eine lange demokratische Tradition.
f. Er spricht Englisch wie ein Engländer.
g. In unserem Hotel wohnten auch einige Engländer.
h. Anstatt eine neue Maschine zu kaufen, ließ er die alte reparieren.
i. Dieses Modell ist mit Abstand das beste, das wir Ihnen anbieten können.
j. Diese Karten waren ziemlich teuer. Ich konnte keine billigeren bekommen.
k. Deutsche Kameras sind teurer als japanische.

look after somebody [luk]	sich um jemanden kümmern
evacuate somebody [i'vækjueit]	jemanden evakuieren
a democratic tradition [demə'krætik]	eine demokratische Tradition
stay at a hotel [həu'tel]	in einem Hotel wohnen
repair a machine [mə'ʃiːn]	eine Maschine reparieren
by far the best model ['mɔdl]	mit Abstand das beste Modell
offer a new model ['ɔfə]	ein neues Modell anbieten
tickets for the theatre ['θiətə]	Karten fürs Theater
an expensive camera [iks'pensiv]	eine teure Kamera

Supply the correct form of the word in brackets.

a. Even (wise) people sometimes act (unwise).
b. The cake didn't taste as (fresh) as a (fresh) baked one.
c. He looked (honest), and he (certain) dealt (honest) with his customers.
d. The after-shave lotion smells very (pleasant), but the soap smells (strange) (sweet).
e. They're coming (dangerous) (near).
f. He (usual) drives (extreme) (fast).
g. A man who takes things (easy) does not (easy) lose his temper.
h. (Admitted) it's (hard) work, and they have to work (hard) to get the job done.
i. He sleeps (sound), gets up (late), does (hard) any work, and tires (quick).
j. He's never been (late) (late).
k. You can live (pretty) (cheap) in this part of the world.
l. She's still (pretty) young, and she's always (pretty) dressed.

you didn't act like a friend [frend]	du hast nicht wie ein Freund gehandelt
an unwise decision [di'siʒn]	eine unkluge Entscheidung
the cake has a strange taste [streinʒ]	der Kuchen hat einen eigenartigen Geschmack
the sauce tastes of garlic [sɔːs]	die Soße schmeckt nach Knoblauch
an honest man ['ɔnist]	ein ehrlicher Mann
a certain Mr Brown ['sɜːtn]	ein gewisser Herr Brown
I'm certain he spoke the truth [truːθ]	ich bin sicher, daß er die Wahrheit gesprochen hat
after-shave lotion ['ləuʃn]	Rasierwasser (für nach der Rasur)
he lost his temper ['tempə]	er verlor die Geduld; er wurde wütend
he admitted the mistake	er gab den Fehler zu
when did you get up this morning?	wann bist du heute morgen aufgestanden?

Please translate.

a. Er ist stärker als ich.
b. Ich wußte nicht, daß er es war.
c. Es hat jemand angerufen. – Wer war es?
d. Wenn der Hund nicht gewesen wäre, wäre ich ertrunken.
e. Es gibt hier nicht viele Füchse.
f. So kann man es nicht machen.
g. Man muß ihn einfach gern haben.
h. Diesen Ausdruck kann man nicht übersetzen.

I phoned him at the office	ich habe ihn im Büro angerufen
he (was) nearly drowned [draund]	er wäre beinahe ertrunken
fox [fɔks]	Fuchs
I like the dog very much [laik]	ich habe den Hund sehr gern
translate an expression [iks'preʃn]	einen Ausdruck übersetzen

Please translate.

a. Er hatte einen Stock in der Hand.
b. Nimm den Finger aus der Nase!
c. Du mußt dir nach jeder Mahlzeit die Zähne putzen.
d. Er nahm sie bei der Hand.
e. Er hat sie ja nur auf die Schulter geküßt.
f. Er will einen eigenen Wagen haben.
g. Dies Haus gehört nicht uns.
h. Er ist ein guter Freund von mir.
i. Meine Aufnahmen sind nicht sehr gut, aber deine sind auch nicht besser.

walk with a stick [wɔ:k]	am Stock gehen
three meals a day [mi:lz]	drei Mahlzeiten pro Tag
tooth [tu:θ] (*pl.* teeth [ti:θ])	Zahn
shoulder ['ʃəuldə]	Schulter
take some photos ['fəutəuz]	einige Aufnahmen machen

Please translate.

a. Hast du dich verletzt?
b. Hast du dich entschuldigt?
c. Wir konnten uns nicht konzentrieren.
d. Wir konnten uns nicht verständlich machen.
e. Sie drehte sich um.
f. Sie sah sich um.
g. Sie können sich nicht verteidigen.
h. Sie können sich nicht bewegen.
i. Er beschwerte sich beim Geschäftsführer.
j. Er stellte sich beim Geschäftsführer vor.

he was badly hurt in the crash [kræʃ]	er wurde bei dem Zusammenstoß schwer verletzt
concentrate ['kɔnsəntreit]	konzentrieren
turn something round [raund]	etwas umdrehen
defend a position [di'fend]	eine Stellung verteidigen
she couldn't move the stone [muːv]	sie konnte den Stein nicht bewegen
manager ['mænidʒə]	Geschäftsführer
can you introduce me to your friend? [intrə'djuːs]	können Sie mich Ihrem Freund vorstellen?

Please translate.

a. Wer hat euch besucht, und wen habt ihr besucht?
b. Wer arbeitet für Sie, und für wen arbeiten Sie?
c. Wer gab Ihnen Geld, und wem haben Sie Geld gegeben?
d. Von wem ist dieser Brief?
e. Von wem wird dieses Produkt vertrieben?
f. Wem gehören diese Kühe?
g. In wessen Haus wird die Versammlung stattfinden?
h. Wovor hast du Angst?
i. Wovon leben diese Menschen?
j. Worauf werden Sie sich spezialisieren?
k. Worüber beklagt er sich?
l. Aus welchem Glas hast du getrunken?
m. Von welchem Smith redest du?
n. Wer von Ihnen fährt zum Bahnhof?

visit somebody ['vizit]	jemanden besuchen
distribute a product [dis'tribju:t ə 'prɔdəkt]	ein Produkt vertreiben
these suitcases belong to me	diese Koffer gehören mir
the meeting took place here	die Versammlung fand hier statt
she's afraid of the dog [ə'freid]	sie hat Angst vor dem Hund
they live mainly on rice [rais]	sie leben hauptsächlich von Reis
we specialize in language books ['speʃəlaiz]	wir sind auf Sprachbücher spezialisiert
he complained about the noise	er beklagte sich über den Lärm
drink from / out of a glass [glɑ:s]	aus einem Glas trinken
talk about somebody [tɔ:k]	über jemanden reden
go to the station ['steiʃn]	zum Bahnhof gehen / fahren

Supply relative pronouns (*who*, *whom*, *whose*, *which*, or *that*) and commas where necessary.

a. You're the only person ...... can help us now.
b. The firm ...... used to supply us with spare parts is no longer there.
c. He's one of the nicest men ...... I've ever met.
d. The English ...... have a long democratic tradition don't use the word *democracy* very often.
e. Henderson ...... many regard as one of our most capable politicians will get an important cabinet post.
f. The cat ...... ate rat poison has been given an injection.
g. The pub ...... you mean is somewhere off Fleet Street.
h. The lawyer to ...... she went for advice did not offer her much encouragement.
i. He used a strange technical term the meaning of ...... I could only guess.
j. The victims four of ...... are in a critical condition are all in St Mary's Hospital.
k. Professor Smith ...... book on animal behaviour you may have read has been awarded the Nobel Prize.
l. They say that dogs ...... bark don't bite, but the dog ...... bit me apparently didn't know that saying.

supply with spare parts [sə'plai]	mit Ersatzteilen beliefern
democracy [di'mɔkrəsi]	Demokratie
regard a man as capable ['keipəbl]	einen Mann für fähig halten
politician [pɔli'tiʃn]	Politiker
off Fleet Street ['ɔf 'fliːt striːt]	in einer Seitenstraße der Fleet Street
encouragement [in'kʌridʒmənt]	Ermutigung
technical term ['teknikl 'təːm]	Fachausdruck
victim of a traffic accident	Opfer eines Verkehrsunfalls
award a prize [ə'wɔːd]	einen Preis zuerkennen / verleihen
bite – bit – bitten	beißen – biß – gebissen
apparently [ə'pærəntli]	anscheinend; offenbar
did you know that saying? [nəu]	kanntest du dieses Sprichwort?

Translate, using contact clauses (i.e., relative clauses without relative pronouns).

a. Er sollte etwas studieren, wofür er sich wirklich interessiert.
b. Der Mann, an den der Brief adressiert ist, ist schon zwei Jahre tot.
c. Er redet dauernd über Dinge, von denen er nichts versteht.
d. Ich bin der einzige Mensch, zu dem er Vertrauen hat.
e. Das Hotel, in dem wir voriges Jahr gewohnt haben, hat seine Preise um 30 Prozent erhöht.
f. Der Film, den sich der Junge gerade ansieht, ist eigentlich nicht für Kinder geeignet.
g. Die Sachen, über die sie jetzt verhandeln, sind von größter Bedeutung.
h. Glücklicherweise war das Fenster, aus dem er sprang, im Erdgeschoß.

is he interested in history? — interessiert er sich für Geschichte?
address a letter to somebody — einen Brief an jemand adressieren
he's constantly making mistakes — er macht dauernd Fehler
he knows nothing about music — er versteht nichts von Musik
have confidence in somebody — zu jemandem Vertrauen haben
stay at a hotel [həu'tel] — in einem Hotel wohnen
they've increased their prices — sie haben ihre Preise erhöht
look at a film [luk] — sich einen Film ansehen
the film is not really suitable for children ['sju:təbl] — der Film ist für Kinder eigentlich nicht geeignet
negotiate (about) something [ni'gəuʃieit] — über etwas verhandeln
of the utmost importance — von größter Bedeutung
fortunately ['fɔ:tʃnitli] — glücklicherweise
jump out of the window [dʒʌmp] — aus dem Fenster springen
on the ground floor [flɔ:] — im Erdgeschoß

Please translate.

a. Ich kenne ihn.
   Ich kenne ihn schon seit Jahren.
b. Ich bin hier.
   Ich bin schon seit zwei Uhr hier.
c. Wir haben ein Auto.
   Wir haben dies Auto schon seit fünf Jahren.
d. Es regnet.
   Es regnet schon seit gestern früh.
e. Spielen Sie Schach?
   Wie lange spielen Sie schon Schach?
f. Wie lange haben Sie schon diese Schmerzen im Bein?
g. Wir verbringen unseren Urlaub meistens an der See.
   Wir verbringen unsere Urlaube schon seit Jahren an der See.
h. Seitdem mich dieser Schäferhund gebissen hat, habe ich Angst vor Hunden.

chess [tʃes]	Schach
this pain in the leg [pein]	diese Schmerzen im Bein
spend a holiday at the seaside ['hɔlədi]	einen Urlaub an der See verbringen
Alsatian [æl'seiʃn]	(deutscher) Schäferhund
bite – bit – bitten	beißen – biß – gebissen
I'm not afraid of dogs [ə'freid]	ich habe keine Angst vor Hunden

Please translate.

a. Dein Paket ist angekommen.
b. Dein Paket ist gerade angekommen.
c. Dein Paket ist gestern früh angekommen.
d. Dein Paket ist heute morgen angekommen.
e. Sind Sie schon mal in England gewesen?
f. Sind Sie voriges Jahr nicht in England gewesen?
g. Ich bin in diesem Sommer in England gewesen.
h. Hast du mein neues Kleid gesehen?
i. Wo hast du dieses Kleid das letzte Mal getragen?
j. Sie hat dieses Kleid bisher noch nie getragen.
k. Wo ist er hingegangen?
l. Er ist schon weggegangen.
m. Er ist heute nachmittag abgereist.
n. Der Zug ist vor einer Minute abgefahren.
o. Der Zug ist in letzter Zeit fast nie pünktlich gewesen.
p. Heute ist der Zug pünktlich gewesen.

parcel ['pɑːsl]	Paket
yesterday morning ['jestədi]	gestern früh
this morning ['mɔːniŋ]	heute morgen
Betty's new dress [njuː]	Bettys neues Kleid
wear [wɛə] – wore [wɔː] – worn [wɔːn]	(z. B. Kleid:) tragen – trug – getragen
leave – left – left	weggehen – wegging – weggegangen; abreisen – abreiste – abgereist
this afternoon ['ɑːftə'nuːn]	heute nachmittag
the train was on time [trein]	der Zug war pünktlich
lately ['leitli]	in letzter Zeit

Choose the correct form.

a. If (you want, you're wanting) to go to Bexley, (you sit, you're sitting) in the wrong train.
b. I hope (I don't keep, I'm not keeping) you from your supper.
c. The uglier a man's legs are, the better (he plays, he's playing) golf.
d. When a stupid man (does, is doing) something he is ashamed of, (he always declares, he is always declaring) it is his duty. (Shaw)
e. What (does John do, is John doing)? – He's in the garden mending the fence.
f. What (does John do, is John doing)? – He's an engineer.
g. Were you (serious, being serious) when you talked about getting married?
h. (Did you mean, Were you meaning) me when you said there was one person too many in the room?
i. (I've meant, I've been meaning) to ask you this question for some time.
j. What (have you done, have you been doing) all these months?
k. Have you (read, been reading) any good books lately?
l. If I was in a hurry, I would not (sit, be sitting) here with you drinking tea.
m. They (had, were having) breakfast when I (came, was coming); they (had, were having) lunch when I (left, was leaving). They seem to (eat, be eating) all the time.
n. We're buried in snow. It must have (snowed, been snowing) all night.

I don't want to keep you from your supper ['sʌpə]	ich möchte Sie nicht vom Abendbrot abhalten
mend the fence [fens]	den Zaun ausbessern / reparieren
engineer [ɛnʒi'niə]	Ingenieur
when are you getting married?	wann heiratet ihr?
lately ['leitli]	in letzter Zeit
bury somebody ['beri]	jemanden begraben

Please translate.

a. Dies ist das ruhigste Zimmer, das ich Ihnen anbieten kann. – Gut, ich nehme es.
b. Ich sehe Sie dann wahrscheinlich am Morgen.
c. Werden wir das Schwimmbecken benutzen dürfen?
d. Wenn du diese Zeilen liest, bin ich tot.
e. Ich bleibe nicht lange weg.
f. Von nun an sage ich die Wahrheit.
g. Werden Sie das Angebot annehmen?
h. Ich fühle, daß etwas passieren wird.
i. Wie lange werden Sie bleiben?
j. Wir gehen schwimmen. Kommst du mit?
k. Die Waschmaschine wird morgen nachmittag geliefert.
l. Wir geben am Sonnabend eine Party.
m. Wir sehen heute abend fern.
n. Wer wird das heutige Konzert dirigieren?
o. Ich reise übermorgen ab.
p. Sicher feiert ihr heute abend.
q. Er fängt morgen früh mit der Arbeit an.
r. Vergessen Sie nicht, daß der Kanzler Sie heute nachmittag erwartet.
s. Ich hoffe, daß Ihnen die Aufführung gefällt.

offer someone a quiet room	jemandem ein ruhiges Zimmer anbieten
that's probably true ['prɔbəbli]	das stimmt wahrscheinlich
swimming pool ['swimiŋ puːl]	Schwimmbecken
the fourth line from the top	die vierte Zeile von oben
tell the truth [truːθ]	die Wahrheit sagen
accept an offer [ək'sept]	ein Angebot annehmen
deliver a washing machine	eine Waschmaschine liefern
watch television ['teliviʒn]	fernsehen
conduct a concert ['kɔnsət]	ein Konzert dirigieren
celebrate a victory ['selibreit]	einen Sieg feiern
start work ['stɑːt 'wəːk]	mit der Arbeit anfangen
a performance of *Hamlet* [pə'fɔːməns]	eine Aufführung des *Hamlet*

Supply the missing forms.

a. If everybody minded their own business, the world (go) round a great deal faster than it does. (Lewis Carroll)

b. If a thing (be) worth doing, it is worth doing badly. (G. K. Chesterton)

c. If *Hamlet* (be) written in these days, it would probably have been called *The Strange Affair at Elsinore*. (J. M. Barrie)

d. If there were no bad people, there (be) no good lawyers. (Charles Dickens)

e. If you (tell) the truth, you don't have to remember anything. (Mark Twain)

f. If God did not exist, it (be) necessary to invent Him. (Voltaire)

g. If the Romans (be) obliged to learn Latin, they would never have found time to conquer the world. (Heinrich Heine)

h. I (never read) a book if it were possible to talk half an hour with the man who wrote it. (Woodrow Wilson)

i. God (not invent) the automobile if he had intended me to walk. (J. E. Morpurgo)

mind your own business! ['biznis]	kümmere dich um deine eigenen Angelegenheiten!
a great deal faster ['fɑːstə]	sehr viel schneller
lawyer ['lɔːjə]	Rechtsanwalt
tell the truth [truːθ]	die Wahrheit sagen
remember something [ri'membə]	sich an etwas erinnern; sich etwas merken
do such things exist? [ig'zist]	gibt es so etwas?
necessary ['nesisəri]	notwendig; nötig
invent something [in'vent]	etwas erfinden
the Romans ['rəumənz]	die Römer
he was obliged to learn it [ə'blaidʒd]	er mußte es lernen
Latin ['lætin]	Latein; das Lateinische
conquer the world ['kɔŋkə]	die Welt erobern
automobile ['ɔːtəməbiːl]	(*U.S.:*) Auto(mobil)

Please translate.

a. Wenn ich nicht so müde wäre, würde ich ein bißchen im Garten arbeiten.
b. Wenn ich du wäre, würde ich nicht mit dem Wagen fahren.
c. Wenn wir zwei Schlüssel hätten, könntest du auch einen haben.
d. Wir hätten wahrscheinlich weniger Ärger gehabt, wenn wir das teurere Modell gekauft hätten.
e. Das Spiel hätte mehr Spaß gemacht, wenn es nicht die ganze Zeit geregnet hätte.
f. Wenn wir zu Hause geblieben wären, hätten wir viel Zeit und Benzin gespart.
g. Wenn wir den früheren Zug gekriegt hätten, wären wir pünktlich angekommen.
h. Wenn der Hund nicht wäre, würden wir eine Wohnung im Stadtzentrum mieten.
i. Wäre der Hund nicht gewesen, so wären wir mit dem Zug gereist.

I'm tired ['taiəd]	ich bin müde
go by car [kɑ:]	mit dem Wagen/Auto fahren
the key to this door [ki:]	der Schlüssel zu dieser Tür
he had a lot of trouble ['trʌbl]	er hatte viel Ärger
the more expensive model ['mɔdl]	das teurere Modell
the game/match was a lot of fun	das Spiel hat viel Spaß gemacht
save petrol ['petrəl]	Benzin sparen
catch (– caught – caught) a train	einen Zug kriegen/erreichen
arrive on time [ə'raiv]	pünktlich ankommen
rent a flat [flæt]	eine Wohnung mieten
the town/city centre ['sentə]	das Stadtzentrum
travel by train ['trævl]	mit dem Zug reisen

Change the following sentences into indirect speech.

> I want a double room. (He said ...)
> He said (that) he wanted a double room.

a. There won't be any further delays. (They promised ...)
b. That can be arranged. (He told me ...)
c. We don't have any plastic ones. (They informed us ...)
d. There's nothing wrong with the book except that it's unreadable.
   (The reviewer wrote ...)
e. We would have to test you first. (They told me ...)
f. There must be a leak somewhere. (He insisted ...)
g. I noticed nothing unusual. (He claimed ...)
h. The Swiss managed to build a lovely country around their hotels.
   (George Orwell once remarked ...)
i. May I come tomorrow? (She asked ...)
j. Everything I know I learnt after I was thirty. (Clemenceau once said ...)
k. Have you known him long? (She asked me ...)
l. When do you expect to be back? (He asked me ...)
m. Where has she gone? (Everybody was wondering ...)
n. How did he manage to get a permit? (Nobody knew ...)
o. The cheque hasn't arrived yet. (He says ...)
p. The material is absolutely waterproof. (The firm claims ...)
q. A rich man's joke is always funny. (He reminded us of the eternal truth
   that ...)
r. It is much easier to be critical than to be correct. (I think it was Disraeli
   who observed ...)

delay [di'lei]	Verzögerung; Verspätung
reviewer [ri'vju:ə]	Kritiker(in); Rezensent(in)
leak [li:k]	Leck; Loch; undichte Stelle
he claimed to be the owner [kleimd]	er behauptete, der Besitzer zu sein
I wonder where he is ['wʌndə]	ich möchte wissen, wo er ist
permit ['pə:mit]	Genehmigung; Erlaubnisschein
absolutely waterproof ['æbsəlu:tli]	vollkommen wasserdicht
eternal [i'tə:nl]	ewig; zeitlos; unabänderlich
Shaw once observed ... [əb'zə:vd]	Shaw bemerkte / äußerte einmal ...

Please translate.

a. Die Fenster werden einmal im Monat geputzt.
b. In der Nähe der Leiche wurde ein schwarzer Regenschirm gefunden.
c. Die Schule wurde im fünfzehnten Jahrhundert von Mönchen gegründet.
d. Sind die Betten gemacht worden?
e. Noch nie zuvor war der Wettbewerb von einer Frau gewonnen worden.
f. Dieses Problem könnte leicht gelöst werden.
g. Ein Teil des Magens mußte entfernt werden.
h. Er wird wahrscheinlich operiert werden müssen.
i. Der Patient wird gerade untersucht.
j. Er vermutete, daß er immer noch beschattet wurde.
k. Von wem wurden diese Fotos gemacht?

clean the windows [kli:n]	die Fenster putzen
(dead) body ['bɔdi]	Leiche; Leichnam
a black umbrella [ʌm'brelə]	ein schwarzer Regenschirm
find [faind] – found [faund] – found [faund]	finden – fand – gefunden
found a school [faund]	eine Schule gründen
in the fifteenth century ['sentʃəri]	im fünfzehnten Jahrhundert
monk [mʌŋk]	Mönch
make the beds [bedz]	die Betten machen
win a competition [kɔmpi'tiʃn]	einen Wettbewerb gewinnen
solve a problem ['prɔbləm]	ein Problem lösen
part of the stomach ['stʌmək]	ein Teil des Magens
remove a stain [ri'mu:v]	einen Fleck entfernen
operate on somebody ['ɔpəreit]	jemanden operieren
examine a patient [ig'zæmin]	einen Patienten untersuchen
suspect [səs'pekt]	argwöhnen; vermuten
shadow somebody ['ʃædəu]	jemanden beschatten
take some photos ['fəutəuz]	einige Fotos machen

Change the following sentences into the passive.

> They advised her to book in advance.
> She was advised to book in advance.

a. She didn't allow him to go swimming.
b. They assured me that the matter would be investigated.
c. You can't expect them to be helpful in any way.
d. Several people had to help the old man up to the platform.
e. A large number of volunteers joined us.
f. They showed her how to operate the machine.
g. Who will succeed him?
h. I told them to be quiet.
i. Can you trust her?

he advised me to stay [əd'vaizd]	er riet mir zu bleiben
book in advance [əd'vɑːns]	im voraus buchen
he assured me I had nothing to fear [ə'ʃuəd]	er versicherte mir, daß ich nichts zu befürchten hätte
investigate a matter [in'vestigeit]	eine Angelegenheit untersuchen
a helpful official [ə'fiʃl]	ein hilfsbereiter Beamter
platform ['plætfɔːm]	Plattform; Podium; Bahnsteig
some volunteers [vɔlən'tiəz]	einige Freiwillige
join a group [gruːp]	sich einer Gruppe anschließen
operate a machine [mə'ʃiːn]	eine Maschine bedienen
Brown succeeded Smith [sək'siːdid]	Brown wurde Smiths Nachfolger
you can trust him [trʌst]	du kannst ihm (ver)trauen; du kannst dich auf ihn verlassen

Change the following sentences into the passive.

> She brought him a cup of tea.
> He was brought a cup of tea.

a. They asked me some questions.
b. He gave her a letter to translate.
c. Somebody handed him a bunch of flowers.
d. She offered us a table by the window.
e. He paid them a satisfactory price.
f. Did they promise you a reward?
g. He showed me some interesting new models.
h. I hope she'll teach him a lesson.

ask somebody a question [ɑːsk]	jemandem eine Frage stellen
translate a letter [træns'leit]	einen Brief übersetzen
hand somebody something [hænd]	jemandem etwas reichen
a bunch of flowers [bʌnʃ]	ein Blumenstrauß
offer somebody something ['ɔfə]	jemandem etwas anbieten
a table by the window ['teibl]	ein Tisch am Fenster
satisfactory [sætis'fæktəri]	befriedigend; zufriedenstellend
promise a reward [ri'wɔːd]	eine Belohnung versprechen
the latest model ['mɔdl]	das neueste Modell
teach somebody a lesson [tiːtʃ]	jemandem eine Lektion erteilen

Please translate.

> Ich weiß nicht, was ich tun soll.
> I don't know what to do.

a. Ich hatte keine Ahnung, was ich sagen sollte.
b. Weißt du, wie man da hinkommt?
c. Er weiß, wie man mit Pferden umgeht.
d. Sie wußte nicht, ob sie lachen oder weinen sollte.
e. Sie weiß, wann sie ihren Mann in Ruhe lassen muß.
f. Wir wissen nicht, wen wir zu unserer Hochzeit einladen sollen.
g. Ich denke darüber nach, welchen Schlips ich anziehen soll.
h. Sie stritten sich darüber, wo sie ihren Urlaub verbringen sollten.

I've no idea [ai'diə]	ich habe keine Ahnung
how did you get here?	wie bist du hierhergekommen?
can you handle a horse? [hɔ:s]	kannst du mit einem Pferd umgehen?
why is that little girl crying?	warum weint das kleine Mädchen da?
you must leave him alone [ə'ləun]	du mußt ihn in Ruhe lassen
invite somebody to a wedding	jemanden zu einer Hochzeit einladen
what are you thinking about?	worüber denkst du nach?
put on a tie [tai]	einen Schlips anziehen
quarrel with somebody ['kwɔrəl]	sich mit jemandem streiten
spend a holiday in Italy ['itəli]	einen Urlaub in Italien verbringen

Please translate.

> Sie ist nicht der Typ, der silberne Löffel stiehlt.
> She's not the type to steal silver spoons.

a. Ich war einer der letzten, die ihn lebend gesehen haben.
b. Ich wäre der erste gewesen, der das zugegeben hätte.
c. Es gibt nichts, das darauf hindeutet, daß der Mörder Linkshänder ist.
d. Er wählte fünf Männer aus, die ihn auf seiner Expedition begleiten sollten.
e. Da ist ein Herr Butler, der Sie sprechen möchte.
f. Sie interessiert sich für alles, was mit seiner Arbeit zu tun hat.
g. Ich werde dir ein Buch geben, das du im Flugzeug lesen kannst.
h. Ich brauche jemand, mit dem ich mich unterhalten kann.
i. Sie sah nichts, worüber sie hätte lachen können.
j. Sie hat nicht gelitten; das ist etwas, wofür man dankbar sein muß.

alive [ə'laiv]	lebend; lebendig; (noch) am Leben
he admitted his mistake [əd'mitid]	er gab seinen Fehler zu
these symptoms indicate severe illness ['indikeit]	diese Symptome deuten auf eine ernste Erkrankung hin
murderer ['mə:dərə]	Mörder
he's left-handed ['left-'hændid]	er ist Linkshänder
choose [tʃu:z] – chose [tʃəuz] – chosen ['tʃəuzn]	(aus)wählen – (aus)wählte – (aus)gewählt
expedition [ekspi'diʃn]	Expedition
accompany somebody [ə'kʌmpəni]	jemanden begleiten
he isn't interested in history ['intristid]	er interessiert sich nicht für Geschichte
talk to somebody [tɔ:k]	sich mit jemandem unterhalten
he suffered from lung cancer	er litt an Lungenkrebs
I'm very grateful to you ['greitful]	ich bin Ihnen sehr dankbar

Noun + infinitive or noun + preposition + *-ing* form?

> He hasn't the courage (say) what he thinks.
> He hasn't the courage to say what he thinks.

> He had the advantage (be) twenty inches taller than Brown.
> He had the advantage of being twenty inches taller than Brown.

a. He lacks the ability (persuade) other people.
b. She made no attempt (conceal) her dislike.
c. He is in no danger (overwork) himself.
d. I don't understand how the boy can take delight (torture) animals.
e. What kept him on his feet was his determination (not give up).
f. He had difficulty (find) paper to write on.
g. He didn't have much experience (change) wheels.
h. For many people freedom seems to mean chiefly the freedom (criticize).
i. It isn't my habit (discuss) my sex life in public.
j. Some people are in the habit (discuss) their sex life in public.
k. We haven't much hope (get) tickets.
l. He gave the impression (be) rather bored.
m. Only one thing was left: the instinct (survive).
n. He hadn't the least intention (do) any more work.
o. He has just announced his intention (retire) at the end of the year.
p. There is no better method (learn) a foreign language.
q. He made up his mind (accept) the offer.
r. He's a busy man and seldom has occasion (leave) London.
s. The annual meeting would be an ideal occasion (discuss) this problem.
t. There would have been no point (continue) the conversation.
u. I'm afraid I'm not in a position (do) anything about it.
v. We look forward to the privilege (welcome) you as our guest.
w. What are your reasons (want) to change your job?
x. He had the reputation (be) a habitual drunkard.
y. The Editor reserves the right (reject or shorten) letters.
z. Because of the serious nature of this offence we are taking the unusual step (send) you to prison.

Verb + infinitive, verb + *-ing* form, or verb + preposition + *-ing* form?

He agreed (wait) for another six weeks.
He agreed to wait for another six weeks.

She enjoys (have) people to dinner.
She enjoys having people to dinner.

I must insist (be) given a replacement.
I must insist on being given a replacement.

---

a. He's admitted (be) in the house at the time of the murder.
b. Some people advocate (begin) sex education at kindergarten level.
c. She can afford (buy) practically anything she sees.
d. Mrs Judy Hunter kindly assisted me (collect) the material for this book.
e. He vainly attempted (continue) the conversation.
f. He doesn't believe (give) the children too much freedom.
g. I can't stand (be) kept waiting.
h. I don't claim (know) everything.
i. He complains (be) treated like a child.
j. I never even considered (join) the party.
k. Once or twice she had debated (start) a small dress business.
l. At last he has decided (start) (look) for a job.
m. She delights (go) to parties.
n. At first he denied (be) in the house, but later he admitted it.
o. She detests (be) told what to do.
p. We'll have to discontinue (water) the lawns because of the water shortage.
q. He dislikes (be) disturbed by the telephone at dinner.
r. Have you finished (repair) the central heating?
s. He couldn't help (regard) her remark as a compliment.
t. We wouldn't hesitate (make) changes if necessary.
u. How can I finish my story if you keep (interrupt) all the time?
v. I object (pay) damages when I'm not at fault.
w. My name's Joan, but he persists (call) me Jean.
x. I now regret (not go) with her when she asked me.
y. Remember (use) the postcode!
z. I specialize (be) right when other people are wrong.

Please translate.

> Ich erwarte, daß du dich anständig benimmst.
> I expect you to behave decently.

a. Erlauben Sie mir, daß ich mich vorstelle.
b. Ich weiß nicht, was ihn veranlaßt hat, seine Entscheidung aufzuschieben.
c. Wir konnten ihn nicht dazu kriegen, einen Mantel anzuziehen.
d. Ich hasse es, wenn mich jemand bei der Arbeit beobachtet.
e. Ich liebe es, wenn du mir abends Geschichten vorliest.
f. Der Offizier befahl seinen Leuten, nicht zu schießen.
g. Ich würde es vorziehen, wenn Sie etwas von Mozart spielten.
h. Erinnere mich bitte daran, die Theaterkarten zu kaufen.
i. Sie sagte mir, ich solle dich an die Geschenke erinnern.
j. Ich vertraue darauf, daß du es taktvoll tust.
k. Warum willst du nicht, daß der Hund auf dem Sofa schläft?

may I introduce myself? [intrə'dju:s]	darf ich mich vorstellen?
what caused him to do that? [kɔ:zd]	was veranlaßte ihn, das zu tun?
postpone a decision [pəust'pəun]	eine Entscheidung aufschieben
put a coat on [kəut]	einen Mantel anziehen
he was watching me work ['wɔtʃiŋ]	er beobachtete mich bei der Arbeit
read somebody a story ['stɔ:ri]	jemandem eine Geschichte vorlesen
officer ['ɔfisə]	Offizier
shoot [ʃu:t] – shot [ʃɔt] – shot	schießen – schoß – geschossen
which do you prefer? [pri'fə:]	welches ziehen Sie vor?
he reminded me of my promise [ri'maindid]	er erinnerte mich an mein Versprechen
theatre tickets ['θiətə]	Theaterkarten
a nice birthday present ['preznt]	ein nettes Geburtstagsgeschenk
you can trust me [trʌst]	Sie können mir vertrauen
tactful(ly) ['tæktful(i)]	taktvoll
sofa ['səufə]	Sofa

Change the following sentences into the passive.

> They allowed him to stay.
> He was allowed to stay.

a. They advised him to go to the Central Library.
b. They asked me to sign the document.
c. Who will they choose to represent us at the conference?
d. He expects the project to move slowly.
e. The oil crisis forced them to shut down their factory.
f. They hired me to do all the dirty work.
g. Can we persuade you to come with us?
h. We told her not to open the door.
i. You must warn the children not to touch the wires.
j. We never heard him speak kindly to his wife.
k. Somebody saw him walk down the High Street.
l. They made the prisoners march to the station.
m. We should make all foreigners feel at home.

he advised me to stay [əd'vaizd]	er riet mir zu bleiben
library ['laibrəri]	Bibliothek
sign a letter [sain]	einen Brief unterzeichnen / unterschreiben
document ['dɔkjumənt]	Dokument; Urkunde
represent a firm [repri'zent]	eine Firma vertreten / repräsentieren
conference ['kɔnfərəns]	Konferenz; Verhandlung
project ['prɔdʒekt]	Projekt; Vorhaben
shut down a factory ['fæktəri]	eine Fabrik schließen / stillegen
hire somebody ['haiə]	jemanden einstellen / anstellen
persuade someone to do something	jemanden bewegen, etwas zu tun
touch an electric wire [tʌtʃ]	eine elektrische Leitung berühren
prisoner ['priznə]	Gefangene(r); Häftling
march along a road [mɑ:tʃ]	eine Straße entlangmarschieren
foreigner ['fɔrinə]	Ausländer(in)

Active or passive? Supply the correct form of the verb in brackets.

> You are to (congratulate) on doing an excellent job.
> You are to be congratulated on doing an excellent job.

> Photography is not hard to (learn).
> Photography is not hard to learn.

a. The Arab oil embargo was not to (foresee).
b. The consequences of the oil embargo are difficult to (foresee).
c. That was a very dangerous thing to (do).
d. The important work is to (do) first.
e. He is always interesting to (talk) to.
f. The reason for these difficulties is not far to (seek).
g. Nothing unusual was to (see).
h. A lot of hard work remains to (do) before we can sit back and relax.
i. Cars are not to (park) in front of the house.
j. He has a wife and two children to (take) care of.
k. The doctor has still got another patient to (see).
l. That threat is not to (take) seriously.
m. Having fed on bad news for so long, he found the good news hard to (believe).
n. A layman might find Manet and Monet easy to (confuse).
o. *Mathematics for the Millions* was a most expensive book to (produce).
p. He left strict orders that the windows were not to (open).
q. The house is definitely not fit to (live) in.
r. The main question is yet to (answer).

congratulate someone on something	jemandem zu etwas gratulieren
foresee – foresaw – foreseen	vorhersehen – -sah – -gesehen
seek [siːk] – sought [sɔːt] – sought	suchen – suchte – gesucht
you ought to relax a little [riˈlæks]	du solltest dich ein bißchen entspannen
take a threat seriously [θret]	eine Drohung ernst nehmen
layman [ˈleimən]	Laie; Nichtfachmann
confuse Manet with Monet [kənˈfjuːz]	Manet mit Monet verwechseln
the house is not fit to live in	das Haus ist unbewohnbar

Please translate.

> Der Arzt bestand darauf, daß das Kind im Bett blieb.
> The doctor insisted on the child staying in bed.

a. Du hast doch nichts dagegen, wenn ich dich Piggy nenne?
b. Ich erinnere mich daran, daß du seinen Namen erwähntest.
c. Ich kann mir nicht vorstellen, daß er je Angst hat.
d. Alles hängt jetzt davon ab, daß sie zu Hause ist.
e. Es hat keinen Sinn, wenn wir uns streiten.
f. Wie hast du es fertiggebracht, sie nach oben zu tragen, ohne daß sie aufwachten?
g. Ich bin es leid, daß mir jeder diese Frage stellt.
h. Ich bin erstaunt darüber, daß ein Mann wie Sie Gerüchten Beachtung schenkt.

do you mind if I smoke? [maind] — haben Sie was dagegen, wenn ich rauche?

we call him Piggy [kɔːl] — wir nennen ihn Piggy

don't you remember me? [ri'membə] — erinnern Sie sich nicht an mich?

his name was not mentioned ['menʃnd] — sein Name wurde nicht erwähnt

can you imagine that? [i'mædʒin] — können Sie sich das vorstellen?

he's afraid of the dog [ə'freid] — er hat Angst vor dem Hund

that depends on the weather [di'pendz] — das hängt vom Wetter ab

why are you always quarrelling? ['kwɔrəliŋ] — warum streitet ihr euch dauernd?

he somehow managed to stay awake ['mænidʒd] — irgendwie brachte er es fertig, wach zu bleiben

upstairs ['ʌp'stɛəz] — nach oben (im Hause)

wake up – woke up – woken up — aufwachen – aufwachte – aufgewacht

I'm sick of this work [wəːk] — ich bin diese Arbeit leid

he asked me some questions [ɑːskt] — er stellte mir einige Fragen

he was surprised at the size of the room [sə'praizd] — er war über die Größe des Zimmers erstaunt

pay attention to rumours ['ruːməz] — Gerüchten Beachtung schenken

Please translate.

> Die Leute, die sich das Spiel anschauten, waren alle begeistert.
> The people watching the match were all enthusiastic.

a. Gibt es einen Bus, der hinauf zur Burg fährt?
b. In jedem dicken Mann ist ein dünner, der herauswill.
c. Die Straße, die die beiden Dörfer verbindet, ist sehr schmal.
d. Die Leute, die diese Arbeit tun, werden äußerst gut bezahlt.
e. Das Geld, das auf dem Tisch liegt, ist für dich.
f. Für jeden, der Englisch lernen möchte, ist dies der schnellste Weg zum Erfolg.
g. Sind Sie sicher, daß es keine weiteren Dokumente gibt, die noch irgendwo herumliegen?
h. Die hier lebenden Menschen sind alle freundlich und hilfsbereit.
i. Die Bombe tötete einen in der Nähe stehenden Polizisten.
j. Die an der Wand hängenden Drucke sind alle von demselben Künstler.

this bus goes up to the castle ['kɑːsl]	dieser Bus fährt hinauf zur Burg
a fat man [fæt]	ein dicker Mann
he wants to get out [wɔnts]	er will heraus
a narrow road ['nærəu]	eine schmale Straße
the road connects two villages	die Straße verbindet zwei Dörfer
success [sək'ses]	Erfolg
document ['dɔkjumənt]	Dokument; Urkunde
he is friendly and helpful	er ist freundlich und hilfsbereit
bomb [bɔm]	Bombe
he was standing nearby ['niə'bai]	er stand (gerade) in der Nähe
he's a policeman [pə'liːsmən]	er ist Polizist
there are some pictures on the wall ['piktʃəz]	es sind einige Bilder an der Wand
he owns some valuable old prints ['væljuəbl]	er besitzt einige wertvolle alte Drucke
artist ['ɑːtist]	Künstler(in)

Please translate.

Er zog den Mantel an und eilte ins Büro.
Putting on his coat, he hurried to the office.

---

a. Sie legte die Zeitung hin und ging in die Küche.
b. Er nahm sie in die Arme und küßte sie.
c. Sie öffnete ihre Handtasche und nahm eine Schachtel Zigaretten heraus.
d. Er stand vor dem Spiegel und rasierte sich mit einem Elektrorasierer.
e. Sie schnitt sich beim Abwaschen in die Hand.
f. Nachdem sie die Tür sorgfältig verschlossen hatte, machte sie Licht und
öffnete das Fenster.
g. Da er sowohl geschickt als auch geduldig war, war er ein gefährlicher
Gegner.
h. Da er nicht Auto fahren kann, fährt er immer mit der Taxe.
i. Da sie sah, daß die Füße des Jungen naß waren, zündete sie ein Feuer
an und zog ihm die Schuhe aus.
j. Da ich großen Hunger hatte, war mir egal, was ich aß.

she put the newspaper down ['nju:speipə]	sie legte die Zeitung hin
handbag ['hænbæg]	Handtasche
a packet of cigarettes ['pækit]	eine Schachtel Zigaretten
mirror ['mirə]	Spiegel
I shave with an electric razor [i'lektrik 'reizə]	ich rasiere mich mit einem Elektrorasierer
she cut her hand [hænd]	sie schnitt sich in die Hand
wash up ['wɔʃ 'ʌp]	abwaschen
lock a door carefully [dɔ:]	eine Tür sorgfältig verschließen
she put on the lights [laits]	sie machte Licht
he's both clever and patient ['peiʃnt]	er ist sowohl geschickt als auch geduldig
he's a dangerous opponent	er ist ein gefährlicher Gegner
he can't drive a car [ka:]	er kann nicht Auto fahren
he always goes by taxi ['tæksi]	er fährt immer mit der Taxe
I don't mind what I eat [maind]	mir ist egal, was ich esse

Please translate.

> Die meisten der hier hergestellten Maschinen werden nach Amerika
> exportiert.
> Most of the machines manufactured here are exported to America.

a. Die in dem Buch enthaltenen Statistiken sind vollkommen veraltet.
b. Einige der von ihm gemachten Vorschläge sind recht vernünftig.
c. Die von dem Ausschuß geleistete Arbeit ist für uns alle von großem
   Wert.
d. Das von Ihnen erwähnte Gespräch fand nicht am dreiundzwanzigsten
   statt.
e. Überall waren mit Maschinengewehren bewaffnete Polizisten zu sehen.
f. Keines der vorgebrachten Argumente war sehr überzeugend.
g. Die neuen Modelle, die auf der Ausstellung gezeigt werden, sind sehr
   interessant.
h. England und Amerika sind zwei Länder, die durch die gleiche Sprache
   getrennt sind.
i. In Camford angekommen, fuhren sie direkt zum Krankenhaus.
j. Obwohl das Buch von den Kritikern gelobt wurde, wurde es nie ein
   Bestseller.
k. Obwohl er offiziell eingeladen wurde, nahm er an der Sitzung nicht teil.

the statistics are out of date	die Statistiken sind veraltet
a reasonable proposal ['riːznəbl]	ein vernünftiger Vorschlag
committee [kə'miti]	Ausschuß; Komitee
mention ['menʃn]	erwähnen
the conversation took place here	das Gespräch fand hier statt
they were armed with machine guns [mə'ʃiːn gʌnz]	sie waren mit Maschinengewehren bewaffnet
put forward an argument ['fɔːwəd]	ein Argument vorbringen
exhibition [eksi'biʃn]	Ausstellung
separate A from B ['sepəreit]	A von B trennen
the critics praised the book	die Kritiker lobten das Buch
he didn't attend the meeting [ə'tend]	er nahm an der Sitzung nicht teil

Please translate.

a. Sie zeigte mir den Brief.
b. Sie zeigte den Brief allen möglichen Leuten.
c. Sie zeigte mir einen Durchschlag des Briefes, den sie ihm geschrieben hatte.
d. Sie zeigte ihn mir.
e. Sie zeigte ihn ihrem Anwalt.
f. Wem zeigte sie den Brief?
g. Wem zeigte sie ihn?
h. Der Brief wurde ihrem Anwalt gezeigt.
i. Warum wurde ihm keine Kopie des Briefes geschickt?
j. Wem wurde der Brief gezeigt?
k. Kannst du mir das erklären?
l. Kann ich Ihnen noch einige weitere Briefe diktieren?
m. Ich hätte das Haus nicht gefunden, wenn du es mir nicht beschrieben hättest.
n. Ich beneide Sie um Ihre wundervolle Stimme.

all sorts of people ['pi:pl]	alle möglichen Leute
a carbon (copy) of the letter ['ka:bn]	ein Durchschlag des Briefes
lawyer ['lɔ:jə]	(Rechts-)Anwalt
a copy of the letter ['kɔpi]	eine Kopie des Briefes
explain a problem to somebody	jemandem ein Problem erklären
dictate letters to somebody [dik'teit]	jemandem Briefe diktieren
describe something to somebody	jemandem etwas beschreiben
envy somebody ['envi]	jemanden beneiden
she has a wonderful voice [vɔis]	sie hat eine wundervolle Stimme

Please translate.

a. Wann haben Sie den Brief abgeschickt?
b. Ich habe den Brief abgeschickt, aber nicht das Paket.
c. Haben Sie ihn abgeschickt?
d. Vergiß nicht, das Wasser abzudrehen.
e. Trink dein Bier aus!
f. Wir haben das ganze Bier im Haus ausgetrunken.
g. Haben Sie die Formulare ausgefüllt, die ich Ihnen gestern gegeben habe?
h. Wenn du ihm Geld leihst, wirst du es nie wiederbekommen.
i. Ich muß versuchen, das Geld wiederzubekommen, das ich ihm geliehen habe.
j. Das Zimmer wird hübscher aussehen, wenn ich alle Bilder aufgehängt habe.
k. Wann wirst du sie aufhängen?

send off a letter ['send 'ɔf]	einen Brief abschicken
parcel ['pɑːsl]	Paket; Päckchen
turn off the water ['wɔːtə]	das Wasser abdrehen
drink up ['drɪŋk 'ʌp]	austrinken
beer [bɪə]	Bier
fill in a form [fɔːm]	ein Formular ausfüllen
lend money to somebody ['mʌni]	jemandem Geld leihen
get back ['get 'bæk]	wiederbekommen
the room looks pretty / nice	das Zimmer sieht hübsch aus
hang up a picture ['pɪktʃə]	ein Bild aufhängen

Please translate.

a. Ein Extremist hat keine Chance, zum Präsidenten gewählt zu werden.
b. Er hofft, zum Präsidenten gewählt zu werden.
c. Der Präsident machte ihn zu seinem engsten Berater.
d. Er wurde gegen seinen Willen zum Helden gemacht.
e. Er ist zum Botschafter in der Schweiz ernannt worden.
f. Man erklärte den ersten Mai zu einem nationalen Feiertag.
g. Ich habe dich immer für meinen Freund gehalten.
h. Man hält dies allgemein für die beste Lösung.

extremist [iks'tri:mist]	Extremist(in)
elect someone to an office [i'lekt]	jemanden in ein Amt wählen
his closest advisers ['kləusist]	seine engsten Berater
against his will [ə'genst]	gegen seinen Willen
I'm not a hero ['hiərəu]	ich bin kein Held
our ambassador to Switzerland [æm'bæsədə]	unser Botschafter in der Schweiz
the newly appointed director [ə'pɔintid]	der neuernannte Direktor
a national holiday ['hɔlədi]	ein nationaler Feiertag
I consider it very important [kən'sidə]	ich halte es für sehr wichtig
that would be the best solution [sə'lu:ʃn]	das wäre die beste Lösung

Please translate.

a. Wollen Sie ihn sehen?
   Können Sie ihn sehen?
b. Wer gab ihm Geld?
   Wem gab er Geld?
c. Wir wollten ihn nicht einladen.
   Wir konnten ihn nicht einladen.
d. Er haßt es, nicht konsultiert zu werden.
   Er hat es nicht gern, wenn man ihn stört.
e. Er lud nicht nur seine Kollegen, sondern auch alle seine Schüler ein.
f. Ist es glatt draußen? – Ich hoffe nicht.
g. Regen Sie sich nicht auf!
   Seien Sie nicht zu großzügig!
h. Ich brauche dir doch nicht zu helfen, oder?
   Ich brauche doch kein Visum, oder?
i. Ladet ihr nicht oft Leute zum Essen ein?
   Habt ihr nicht oft Gäste?
   Habt ihr ihn denn nicht informiert?

invite someone to lunch [lʌnʃ]	jemanden zum Mittagessen ein- laden
consult somebody [kən'sʌlt]	jemanden konsultieren
please don't disturb him [dis'tə:b]	bitte störe ihn nicht
colleague ['kɔli:g]	Kollege; Kollegin
student ['stju:dənt]	Student(in); Studierende(r); Schüler(in); Kursteilnehmer(in)
the road is slippery ['slipəri]	die Straße ist glatt
get excited / upset [ik'saitid]	sich aufregen
generous ['dʒenərəs]	großzügig
visa ['vi:zə]	Visum; Sichtvermerk
inform somebody [in'fɔ:m]	jemanden informieren

Please translate.

a. Haben wir Milch im Haus?
b. Hat er gestern abend ein Bad genommen?
c. Wir haben den Mörder noch nicht.
d. Haben Sie noch Geschwister?
e. Wann frühstückt ihr normalerweise?
f. Haben Sie viele Diebstähle?
g. Hast du denn keinen Stolz?
h. Hast du um diese Jahreszeit nicht meistens eine Erkältung?
i. Wie viele Junge haben diese Tiere im allgemeinen?
j. Warum habt ihr euch im Garten kein Schwimmbad bauen lassen?

have a bath [bɑːθ]	ein Bad nehmen
murderer ['məːdərə]	Mörder
brothers and sisters ['brʌðəz]	Geschwister
have breakfast ['brekfəst]	frühstücken
usually / normally ['juːʒuəli]	normalerweise; im allgemeinen
theft [θeft]	Diebstahl
wound someone's pride [wuːnd]	jemandes Stolz verletzen
at this time of (the) year	um diese Jahreszeit
have a cold [kəuld]	eine Erkältung haben
an animal and its young ['æniməl]	ein Tier und seine Jungen
swimming pool ['swimiŋ puːl]	Schwimmbecken; Schwimmbad

Please translate.

a. Mögen Sie diese Art von Musik? – Ja. / Nein.
b. Kann sie schwimmen? – Ja. / Nein.
c. Mir gefällt diese Musik sehr. – Mir auch.
d. Ich könnte jetzt einen Scotch vertragen. – Ich auch.
e. Ich kann ihn nicht ausstehen. – Ich auch nicht.
f. Wir sehen nie fern. – Wir auch nicht.
g. Ich liebe dich, Brigitte! – Ich dich auch, George!
h. Wer könnte den Jungen am Flughafen abholen? – Tante Alice könnte es.
i. Ich habe nichts gegen Mäuse. – Aber ich!
j. Warum hast du ihn nicht benachrichtigt? – Aber ich habe es ja!

I like this kind of music ['kaind əv 'mju:zik]	ich mag diese Art von Musik
I enjoy this music [in'dʒɔi]	mir gefällt diese Musik
I could do with a Scotch now [skɔtʃ]	ich könnte jetzt einen Scotch vertragen
I can't stand him [stænd]	ich kann ihn nicht ausstehen
we often watch television ['teliviʒn]	wir sehen oft fern
go to meet someone at the airport	jemanden am Flughafen abholen
mouse [maus] (*pl.* mice [mais])	Maus
I don't mind mice [maind]	ich habe nichts gegen Mäuse
inform somebody [in'fɔːm]	jemanden benachrichtigen

Add question tags to the following sentences.

> You arrived yesterday, ...?
> You arrived yesterday, didn't you?

a. The doctor will come back in the morning, ...?
b. I behaved disgracefully to you, ...?
c. He's got a secretary now, ...?
d. The soup's getting cold, ...?
e. That's a Cadillac, ...?
f. So much has happened suddenly, ...?
g. I'm a lousy player, ...?
h. She always used to call him John, ...?
i. He ought to have won, ...?
j. You don't enjoy this sort of thing, ...?
k. I shouldn't be speaking to you like this, ...?
l. We don't get bored, darling, ...?
m. You can't remember a thing, ...?
n. I'm not wrong, ...?
o. She doesn't like it, ...?
p. You didn't mind me shouting, ...?
q. There's nothing going on, ...?
r. We'll never know, ...?
s. Rita, I don't think you've ever met my mother, ...?
t. Let's play billiards, ...?
u. Let's have a game of chess, ...?
v. Come and sit down, dear, ...?

behave disgracefully [bi'heiv]	sich schändlich benehmen
get cold ['get 'kəuld]	kalt werden
Cadillac ['kædilæk]	(amerikanische Automarke)
a lousy player ['lauzi]	ein miserabler Spieler
get bored [bɔːd]	sich langweilen
there's nothing going on	es tut sich nichts
have you met Rita? ['riːtə]	kennen Sie Rita?
billiards ['biljədz]	Billard(spiel)
have a game of chess [tʃes]	eine Partie Schach spielen

Change the following sentences in the way indicated.

> She had *hardly* arrived when she set out for a look around town.
> *Hardly* had she arrived when she set out for a look around town.

a. They had *hardly* shaken hands when they started quarrelling.
b. We had *hardly* arrived at the theatre when I realized I'd left the tickets at home.
c. You had *scarcely* left when the trouble started.
d. The shooting had *no sooner* begun than Busty fell flat on his face with remarkable speed.
e. Mr Davies *no sooner* got home than he had a very bad pain in his chest.
f. The parents *never* interfered in their son's affairs.
g. I have *rarely* met such generous people.
h. He *only now* became conscious of all that he had forgotten.
i. They can see you *only if you're moving*.
j. He tried *in vain* to get his neighbours to help him.

they set out early ['ə:li]	sie brachen früh auf
he never fully realized that	das wurde ihm nie ganz klar
he had scarcely left ['skɛəsli]	er war gerade erst weggegangen
no sooner ... than ['su:nə]	kaum ... als
with remarkable speed	mit bemerkenswerter Schnelligkeit
he has a bad pain in his chest [tʃest]	er hat starke Schmerzen in der Brust
interfere in someone's affairs [ɪntə'fiə]	sich in jemandes Angelegenheiten einmischen
a generous man ['dʒenərəs]	ein großzügiger Mann
become conscious of a problem ['kɔnʃəs]	sich eines Problems bewußt werden
please don't move [mu:v]	bewege dich bitte nicht
it was all in vain [vein]	es war alles vergebens / vergeblich
can't you get him to help you?	kannst du ihn nicht dazu bekommen, daß er dir hilft?

Please translate.

a. Nachdem unsere Gäste gegangen waren, tranken wir noch eine Flasche Wein.
b. Der Junge wird immer vernünftiger.
c. Da du die Browns nicht magst, werden wir sie nicht einladen.
d. Du redest, als wärest du mein Vater.
e. Du kannst dir die alberne Fernseh-Show ansehen, solange du von mir nicht erwartest, daß ich sie mir auch ansehe.
f. Dieses Problem packen wir an, sobald wir zurückkommen.
g. Bis wir in Urlaub gehen, wird die Operation vergessen sein.
h. Wir werden das Haus bauen, auch wenn sich die Situation verschlechtert.
i. Ich bezweifle, daß das die ganze Wahrheit ist.
j. Nehmt eine Straßenkarte mit für den Fall, daß ihr euch verfahrt.
k. Wenn du erst mal wieder zu Hause bist, kannst du dir all diese Schallplatten anhören.
l. Angenommen, wir gewinnen eine Million im Fußballtoto, würde das genügen, um unsere Schulden zu bezahlen?
m. Die Miete kann ich erst nächste Woche bezahlen.
n. Immer wenn ich in London bin, gehe ich in ein chinesisches Restaurant in der Gerrard Street.
o. Er kam, während wir weg waren.

another bottle of wine ['bɔtl]	noch eine Flasche Wein
he's a sensible boy ['sensəbl]	er ist ein vernünftiger Junge
I don't like the Browns [laik]	ich mag die Browns nicht
watch a silly TV show [wɔtʃ]	sich eine alberne Fernseh-Schau ansehen
tackle / attack a problem [ə'tæk]	ein Problem anpacken
the situation got worse [wə:s]	die Situation verschlechterte sich
take a road map along [ə'lɔŋ]	eine Straßenkarte mitnehmen
we've lost our way [lɔst]	wir haben uns verfahren
listen to a record ['rekɔ:d]	sich eine Schallplatte anhören
win a million on the football pools ['futbɔ:l]	eine Million im Fußballtoto gewinnen
pay the rent [pei]	die Miete bezahlen
a Chinese restaurant ['tʃai'ni:z]	ein chinesisches Restaurant

Supply prepositions where necessary.

a. How much money do you have ...... your bank account ...... the moment?
b. The concert is to be broadcast ...... the afternoon / evening / morning of the 25th December.
c. I'm sure he'll apologize ...... you the moment he realizes he offended you.
d. Why don't you apply ...... a position ...... the export department?
e. We arrived ...... home at noon.
f. Since you've been ...... hospital she's asked / inquired ...... you every day.
g. He doesn't believe ...... doing things by halves.
h. Mary loves chocolate and toffees, but her sister doesn't care ...... sweets at all.
i. Can't we dine out ...... a change?
j. He wrote out a cheque ...... £28.
k. My brother is clever ...... making things with his hands, but I am not.
l. I'll lend you the money ...... condition that you repay it within six weeks.
m. If you torture a man, he'll confess ...... crimes he never committed.
n. I can only congratulate you ...... the way you handled that delicate situation.
o. The book consists ...... twenty-four chapters.
p. In America, a haberdasher deals ...... men's hats, shirts, neckties, gloves, and so on.
q. His latest book deals ...... living conditions in some South American countries.
r. What did the cat die ...... ?
s. Brahms' symphonies differ considerably ...... Beethoven's.
t. You look very elegant ...... that brown dress.
u. He enclosed a cheque ...... the letter.
v. He's engaged / married ...... a local girl.
w. Isn't he entitled ...... an old-age pension?
x. How much I envy you ...... going to London!
y. We're all excited ...... having you here.
z. They didn't go out ...... fear ...... being seen.

Supply prepositions where necessary.

a. Being an emancipated woman, she is not frightened ...... expressing her opinions quite definitely.
b. Why don't you go ...... a walk in the park?
c. He's seriously ill ...... jaundice.
d. The dog is jealous ...... the baby.
e. Why don't you join us ...... a game of skat?
f. He didn't finish the composition ...... lack of time.
g. The people here live mainly ...... rice.
h. I've been looking ...... my gloves ...... half an hour, but I can't find them.
i. He says this music doesn't have an emancipatory effect, but I don't know what he means ...... that.
j. I have a feeling that fate means well ...... us.
k. I'm sure this arrangement will meet ...... your approval.
l. She's an interior decorator ...... occupation / profession.
m. She had to be operated .... cancer.
n. Athletes ...... fifteen nations took part ...... the race.
o. They paid ...... the latest shipment ...... cheque.
p. By the time I've paid ...... all the craftsmen I'll be broke.
q. ...... this photo / picture she looks much older than she is.
r. She takes great pride ...... her dog's ability to stand on his hind legs, but I'm sure that's nothing ...... the ordinary.
s. I heard an excellent performance of Gershwin's *Porgy and Bess* ...... the radio the other day.
t. ...... regard ...... your application ...... credit we are still waiting ...... instructions ...... Head Office.
u. Do you think it'll be possible to replace oil ...... coal here?
v. We sail / leave / start ...... Cape Town tomorrow.
w. The whole house smells ...... paint.
x. This shop specializes ...... eighteenth-century English furniture.
y. You use much less petrol if you drive ...... this speed.
z. He obviously suffers ...... an inferiority complex.

Supply prepositions where necessary.

a. She looked quite surprised ...... seeing me.
b. In a typical crime thriller none of the characters is ...... suspicion.
c. People here are deeply suspicious ...... any newcomer.
d. There's an old Garbo film ...... television tonight.
e. Not all husbands are ...... bad terms with their mothers-in-law.
f. The train will arrive at 8.15 if it is ...... time.
g. Are you going there ...... train or ...... car?
h. He was trembling / was shaking / was white ...... fear.
i. This way of dealing ...... the crisis is typical ...... the President.
j. We'll certainly want a room with a view ...... the sea.
k. ...... view ...... the economic situation our plans ...... expansion may have to be reconsidered.
l. Our general manager has just left ...... a visit ...... our Dublin branch.
m. "I wouldn't exactly call him timid," she said ...... a low voice.
n. My grandfather is always waiting ...... something sensational to happen.
o. The room won't look cosy as long as there are no pictures ...... the walls.
p. Welcome ...... England, darling!
q. Welcome ...... home, darling!
r. ...... the whole we can be satisfied with last year's results.
s. The blue whale is now the largest animal ...... the world.

crime thriller ['kraim 'θrilə]	Krimi
reconsider a plan [ri:kən'sidə]	einen Plan (nochmals) über-denken
general manager ['mænidʒə]	Generaldirektor
our Dublin branch [brɑ:nʃ]	unsere Filiale in Dublin
a timid person ['timid]	ein schüchterner / zaghafter Mensch
a cosy room ['kəuzi]	ein gemütliches Zimmer
I'm not satisfied with it ['sætisfaid]	ich bin nicht damit zufrieden
blue whale ['blu: 'weil]	Blauwal

Please translate.

a. Dieses Problem tauchte erstmals gegen Ende des Krieges auf.
b. Es haben sich einige ernste Schwierigkeiten eingestellt.
c. Sie hatte ihm fünf Söhne geboren. Der letzte wurde am 8. März 1812 geboren.
d. Bis jetzt hat er mich im Schach noch nie geschlagen.
e. Das Buch war in Leder gebunden.
f. Hat der Hund Sie schon mal gebissen? – Ja, als er jung war, hat er mich manchmal gebissen.
g. Irgend jemand muß die Kerzen ausgeblasen haben.
h. Du hättest dir leicht den Hals brechen können!
i. Das Programm wurde am vergangenen Freitag gesendet.
j. Die Polizei hat die Entführer gefangen.
k. Der Ring, den sie auswählte, kostete ein kleines Vermögen.
l. In seinem neuesten Buch hat er sich mit diesem Problem ausführlich befaßt.
m. Ich habe an den Feiertagen zuviel gegessen.
n. Ich habe mich noch nie besser als jetzt gefühlt.
o. Er hat an vielen Fronten gekämpft.
p. Als er gestern nach München flog, benahm er sich so, als ob er noch nie vorher geflogen sei.
q. Ich habe meinen Mantel aufgehängt.
r. Im Mittelalter wurden Diebe häufig aufgehängt.
s. Hier sind die fünf Pfund, die du mir vorigen Sonntag geliehen hast.
t. Die Lebenshaltungskosten sind voriges Jahr erheblich gestiegen.
u. Ich habe meine Uhr heute morgen nach der Bahnhofsuhr gestellt.
v. Das Gerücht verbreitete sich schnell.
w. Die Uhr hat gerade geschlagen.
x. Sei vorsichtig, ich habe gerade den Fußboden gefegt!
y. Im Jahre 1940 schwamm ein dreißigjähriger amerikanischer Metzger 292 Meilen in 89 Stunden und 48 Minuten.
z. Ich bin heute morgen um fünf Uhr aufgewacht. Ich wünschte, ich wäre nicht so früh aufgewacht.

Please translate.

a. Darf ich Sie an Ihr Versprechen erinnern?
b. Darf ich dich einen Augenblick unterbrechen? – Nein, das darfst du nicht!
c. Ich darf nicht soviel rauchen.
d. Du darfst nicht immer Versprechungen machen, die du nicht halten kannst.
e. Warum durfte er nicht länger bleiben?
f. Werden wir den großen Saal benutzen dürfen?
g. Wir hoffen, den großen Saal benutzen zu dürfen.
h. Bisher hat sie ihn noch nicht besuchen dürfen.
i. Diese Art von Maschine dürfte leicht zu installieren sein.
j. Du hättest nicht so schnell aufgeben dürfen.

remind someone of a promise ['prɔmis]	jemanden an ein Versprechen erinnern
interrupt somebody [intə'rʌpt]	jemanden unterbrechen
make / keep a promise ['prɔmis]	ein Versprechen machen / halten
a large hall [hɔ:l]	ein großer Saal
so far ['səu 'fɑ:]	bisher
install a machine [mə'ʃi:n]	eine Maschine installieren
give up hope [həup]	die Hoffnung aufgeben

Please translate.

a. Können Sie etwas von Brahms spielen?
b. Können Sie Französisch?
c. Kann man die Maschine nicht reparieren?
d. Er kann das Loch nicht selbst gegraben haben.
e. Sie konnte den Stein nicht vom Boden heben.
f. Sie konnten das Haus zu einem angemessenen Preis verkaufen.
g. Könnten wir nicht auch mit dem Zug fahren?
h. Ich konnte schon mit fünf Jahren schwimmen.
i. Wir könnten auch ohne Öl zurechtkommen.
j. Sie sagte, sie könne mir nicht helfen.
k. Dies könnte mein Schirm sein.
l. Der Zug kann Verspätung gehabt haben.
m. Es kann sein, daß der Zug nicht pünktlich ist.
n. Der Zug hätte Verspätung haben können.
o. Ich hätte das Kaninchen nicht töten können.
p. Er dachte, die Tabletten könnten vielleicht helfen.
q. Wir werden nicht mit dem Auto fahren können.
r. Er scheint den Text nicht übersetzen zu können.

repair a machine [məˈʃiːn]	eine Maschine reparieren
dig [dig] – dug [dʌg] – dug	graben – grub – gegraben
lift a stone off the ground	einen Stein vom Boden heben
a reasonable price [ˈriːznəbl]	ein angemessener Preis
go by train [trein]	mit dem Zug fahren
get along without oil [əˈlɔŋ]	ohne Öl zurechtkommen
the train was late [leit]	der Zug hatte Verspätung
rabbit [ˈræbit]	Kaninchen
have you taken your tablets? [ˈtæblits]	hast du deine Tabletten ge-nommen?
go by car [kɑː]	mit dem Auto fahren
translate a text [trænsˈleit]	einen Text übersetzen

Please translate.

a. Sie können Ihren Mantel hier lassen.
b. Warum laßt ihr immer die Türe auf?
c. Laß den Hund in Frieden!
d. Er wollte eine Rede halten, aber sie ließen ihn nicht.
e. Sie wird den Jungen nicht gehen lassen.
f. Der Lehrer ließ uns das Gedicht auswendig lernen.
g. Sie ließ die Fensterrahmen grün streichen.
h. Wir werden den Hund impfen lassen müssen.
i. Wir versuchen, unsere Patienten nicht zu lange warten zu lassen.
j. Wenn es nicht besser wird, müssen wir den Arzt kommen lassen.

coat [kəut]	Mantel
make a speech [spiːtʃ]	eine Rede halten
learn a poem by heart ['pəuim]	ein Gedicht auswendig lernen
paint the window frames green	die Fensterrahmen grün streichen
vaccinate somebody ['væksineit]	jemanden impfen
patient ['peiʃnt]	Patient; Patientin
it will soon get better [suːn]	es wird bald besser werden

Please translate.

a. Du könntest wenigstens versuchen, einen guten Eindruck zu machen.
b. Machen Sie es sich bitte bequem!
c. Ich habe mir gerade einen neuen Anzug machen lassen.
d. Sie hat ihn zu einem glücklichen Menschen gemacht.
e. Ich habe noch nicht die Betten gemacht.
f. Wann machst du das Schlafzimmer?
g. Wenn man mit den Leuten hier Geschäfte machen will, muß man Geduld haben.
h. Ich weiß nicht, was ich machen soll.
i. Hat der Junge seine Hausaufgaben gemacht?
j. Was macht dein Vater? (= Wie geht es ihm?)
k. Sie macht jeden Morgen einen langen Spaziergang.
l. Die Schmerzen machen mich wahnsinnig.
m. Das macht nichts!
n. Es ist Zeit, daß ich mich an die Arbeit mache.
o. Drei Flaschen zu je 70 Pence – das macht zwei Pfund zehn.

a good impression [im'preʃn]	ein guter Eindruck
a comfortable chair ['kʌmftəbl]	ein bequemer Sessel / Stuhl
a new suit [sjuːt]	ein neuer Anzug
he's a happy man [mæn]	er ist ein glücklicher Mensch
bedroom ['bedrum]	Schlafzimmer
patience ['peiʃns]	Geduld
this is my homework ['həumwəːk]	dies sind meine Hausaufgaben / Hausarbeiten
a long walk [wɔːk]	ein langer Spaziergang
he's in great pain [pein]	er hat große Schmerzen
are you crazy / mad? ['kreizi]	bist du wahnsinnig?
three bottles at 70 pence each	drei Flaschen zu je 70 Pence

Please translate.

a. Ich habe es tun müssen.
b. Er muß es getan haben.
c. Ich muß jeden Morgen um halb acht im Büro sein.
d. Ich muß morgen vormittag zum Arzt.
e. Es muß geregnet haben.
f. Wir müssen alle unsere Pflicht tun.
g. Wir müssen in Crewe umsteigen.
h. Du mußt nicht immer so grob zu ihm sein!
i. Sie können am Gottesdienst teilnehmen, aber Sie müssen es nicht.
j. Ich fürchte, ich werde jetzt gehen müssen.
k. Sie wird noch mindestens vierzehn Tage im Krankenhaus bleiben müssen.
l. Er mußte sofort operiert werden.
m. Das hätte er eigentlich wissen müssen.

tomorrow morning [tə'mɔrəu]	morgen vormittag; morgen früh
he did his duty ['dju:ti]	er tat seine Pflicht
change at Crewe [kru:]	in Crewe umsteigen
a rude fellow [ru:d]	ein grober Kerl
attend a service [ə'tend]	an einem Gottesdienst teilnehmen
stay in hospital ['hɔspitl]	im Krankenhaus bleiben
operate on somebody ['ɔpəreit]	jemanden operieren

Please translate.

a. Du sollst ihn sofort anrufen.
b. Der Chef soll nicht gestört werden.
c. Wir sollten ihn nie wiedersehen.
d. Was soll das heißen?
e. Diese Zeichnung soll von Picasso sein.
f. Der nächste Winter soll sehr kalt werden.
g. Das Hotel soll eines der teuersten an der Südküste sein.
h. Soll ich die Büchsen in den Kühlschrank tun?
i. Das soll nicht wieder passieren!
j. Man sollte nie zuviel versprechen.
k. Die Stiefel sollten eigentlich dicht sein.
l. Wenn irgend etwas passieren sollte, rufen Sie mich bitte sofort an.
m. Sie sagte, ich solle hier auf sie warten.
n. Wir hätten einen Fachmann befragen sollen.
o. Du hättest die Fenster nicht offenlassen sollen.

phone somebody [fəun]	jemanden anrufen
disturb somebody [dis'tə:b]	jemanden stören
I've never seen him again [ə'gen]	ich habe ihn nie wiedergesehen
what does this word mean? [mi:n]	was heißt dieses Wort?
a drawing by Picasso ['drɔ:iŋ]	eine Zeichnung von Picasso
a tin of corned beef ['kɔ:nd 'bi:f]	eine Büchse Corned beef
refrigerator [ri'fridʒəreitə] ⎫	
fridge [fridʒ] ⎭	Kühlschrank
what's happened? ['hæpnd]	was ist passiert?
he promised to come ['prɔmist]	er versprach zu kommen
these boots are watertight [bu:ts]	diese Stiefel sind (wasser)dicht
wait for somebody [weit]	auf jemanden warten
consult an expert ['ekspə:t]	einen Fachmann befragen
leave the windows open [li:v]	die Fenster offenlassen

Please translate.

a. Ich hoffe, du wirst bald wieder gesund.
b. Ich wurde bei der Rede so müde, daß ich die Augen nicht offenhalten konnte.
c. Es wurde gerade dunkel, als wir ankamen.
d. Wenn meine Sekretärin krank wird, bin ich aufgeschmissen.
e. Es wird heiß heute.
f. Sein ältester Sohn wird wahrscheinlich Musiker.
g. Sein ältester Sohn ist Musiker geworden.
h. Was wird aus dem Hund, wenn die alte Frau stirbt?
i. Sein Haar ist über Nacht weiß geworden.
j. Mein Kaffee ist kalt geworden.
k. Ich würde wahnsinnig, wenn ich hier arbeiten müßte.
l. Die Tage werden kürzer / länger.

you must keep your eyes open — du mußt die Augen offenhalten
if that happens, we'll be in an awful fix ['ɔːfl] — wenn das passiert, sind wir aufgeschmissen
his eldest son ['eldist] — sein ältester Sohn
musician [mju'ziʃn] — Musiker
he stayed away overnight [steid] — er blieb über Nacht fort
he must be crazy / mad ['kreizi] — er muß wahnsinnig sein

Please translate.

a. Alle für einen, einer für alle.
b. Alle Lampen waren an.
c. Alle wußten, wo er sich versteckte.
d. Er bekommt alle zwei Stunden eine Spritze.
e. Er scheint wirklich alles zu wissen.
f. Das Leben hier ist alles andere als angenehm.
g. Sagen Sie bitte die Wahrheit – die ganze Wahrheit und nichts als die Wahrheit!
h. Sie hinterließ ihr ganzes Geld dem Londoner Zoo.
i. Er ist ein ganz anderer Mensch, wenn seine Frau nicht bei ihm ist.
j. Im (großen) ganzen ist unsere Situation nicht schlechter als voriges Jahr.
k. Das Ganze war ein Bluff.
l. Jeder wußte, was er zu tun hatte.
m. Jeder von ihnen wußte, was auf dem Spiel stand.
n. Jede Hausfrau braucht Persil.
o. Sie können mich jederzeit anrufen.
p. Das kann jeder sagen!
q. Leider hatten wir überhaupt kein Geld.
r. Ich brauche keine Ratschläge von Ihnen.
s. Keiner weiß, was er damit gemeint hat.
t. Keiner von uns wußte eine Antwort auf diese Frage.
u. Keiner der beiden Vorschläge scheint akzeptabel zu sein.
v. Ich würde keinen von beiden einladen.

hide [haid] – hid [hid] – hidden	verstecken – versteckte – versteckt
get an injection [in'dʒekʃn]	eine Spritze bekommen
the London Zoo ['lʌndən 'zu:]	der Londoner Zoo
bluff [blʌf]	Bluff; bluffen
there's a lot at stake [steik]	es steht eine Menge auf dem Spiel
housewife ['hauswaif]	Hausfrau
call / phone / ring somebody [fəun]	jemanden anrufen
an acceptable proposal [ək'septəbl prə'pəuzl]	ein akzeptabler Vorschlag

Put in *very* or (*very*) *much* to express the idea of German *sehr*.

a. She's a ...... attractive girl.
   He loves her ......
   They're ...... in love.
b. He may come by the next train, but I doubt it ......
   The outcome of the election is still ...... in doubt.
   The future looks ...... doubtful.
c. He was ...... interested in the story.
   The story interested him ......
   He found the story ...... interesting.
d. We'd like ...... to see the film.
   We're ...... anxious to get tickets for the show.
e. He is ...... respected by all his neighbours.
   He is a ...... respected member of the community.
f. During the last few years language labs have been ...... improved and
   brought into general use.

an attractive girl [ə'træktiv]	ein attraktives Mädchen
I doubt if that is true [daut]	ich bezweifle, daß das wahr ist
a doubtful future ['dautful]	eine ungewisse / unsichere Zukunft
I'm not interested in money ['intristid]	ich bin nicht an Geld interessiert; ich habe kein Interesse an Geld
I'm anxious to get tickets ['æŋkʃəs]	mir liegt daran, Karten zu bekommen
he is respected by everybody [ris'pektid]	er wird von jedermann respektiert / geachtet
neighbour ['neibə]	Nachbar(in)
a member of the community [kə'mju:niti]	ein Mitglied der Gemeinschaft
during the last few years [fju:]	in den letzten Jahren
language lab ['læŋgwidʒ læb]	Sprachlabor
improve something [im'pru:v]	etwas verbessern
in general use ['dʒenərəl 'ju:s]	in allgemeinem Gebrauch

Put in *some* or *any*.

a. Won't you have ...... tea? – No, thanks, I couldn't drink ......thing at the moment, but I'll have ...... tea later if you don't mind.
b. Would you like ......thing to eat? – No, thank you, I had ......thing on the train.
c. Can I offer you ......thing? – Yes, do you happen to have ...... whisky in the house? Scotch is ......thing I really care for after a long walk.
d. I don't think there's ......thing to worry about at this point. But if you have ......difficulty, let me know.
e. I can't see ......body laughing. Did I say ......thing serious for a change?
f. You look upset. Is ......thing wrong? Did I do ......thing you didn't like? Why don't you say ......thing?
g. Isn't there ......thing else you can do besides read the damn newspapers all day? Don't you have ...... hobbies? You can do ......-thing you like, but don't just sit there reading the News of the World!
h. You can come ...... time you like, but do bring ......thing to write.
i. We may regret this decision ...... day, but for the time being ...... decision is better than no decision at all.

I don't care for wine [wain]	ich mache mir nichts aus Wein
difficulty ['difikəlti]	Schwierigkeit
can't we sing a song for a change? [tʃeinʒ]	können wir zur Abwechslung nicht mal ein Lied singen?
he looks upset [ʌp'set]	er sieht verstört aus
the damn newspapers [dæm]	die verdammten Zeitungen
regret a decision [di'siʒn]	eine Entscheidung bereuen / bedauern
for the time being ['bi:iŋ]	fürs erste; unter den gegen-wärtigen Umständen

Read and / or write out the following figures.

a. $\frac{1}{2}$, $2\frac{1}{2}$; $5\frac{1}{3}$, $\frac{2}{3}$; $\frac{1}{4}$, $7\frac{3}{4}$, $\frac{5}{4}$; $\frac{1}{5}$, $\frac{2}{5}$, $\frac{3}{5}$; $9\frac{1}{6}$, $\frac{4}{6}$, $3\frac{5}{6}$.

b. $\frac{1}{50}$, $\frac{2}{25}$; $\frac{85}{250}$, $\frac{193}{477}$.

c. 10.563, 10,563; 7.85, 7,850.

d. 4, 14, 40; 5, 15, 50; 8, 18, 80.

e. 100, 106, 116, 127.

f. 1,236, 1,379; 5,978, 24,932, 100,000, 1,000,000.

g. (Years:) 1066, 1512, 1810, 1974.

h. (Telephone numbers:) 606 3030, 370 4933, 235 7040;
   581-8100, 677-3100, 889-4310.

Read out the following dates.

a. January 1, 1974   July 27, 1955
b. 2 February 1936   28 August 1899
c. March 3, 1960   September 29, 2000
d. 4th April 1900   30th October 1980
e. 25.5.73   22.11.72
f. 6.21.70   12.23.49

SCHLÜSSEL ZU DEN ÜBUNGEN

Zur Beachtung: Ein Schrägstrich (/) trennt jeweils gleichwertige Alternativkonstruktionen.

---

1. Pluralform
a. aircraft. **b.** children. **c.** fish. **d.** feet. **e.** leaves. **f.** mice. **g.** pence. **h.** policemen. **i.** sheep. **j.** teeth.

---

2. Singular- oder Pluralsubstantiv?
a. His advice was not followed / acted upon. **b.** The contents of the cases were not damaged. **c.** The furniture is being delivered tomorrow. **d.** Your glasses are on the table in the living room. **e.** The goods have just arrived. **f.** Here is some important information. **g.** His knowledge of French is limited. **h.** Considerable progress has been made. **i.** The stairs are too steep for the dog. **j.** These trousers / pants / shorts were rather expensive.

---

3. Singular- oder Pluralverb?
a. is. **b.** is. **c.** is. **d.** was. **e.** has. **f.** are. **g.** were. **h.** faces.

---

4. Mit oder ohne the?
a. the. **b.** He says that life is pleasant in Switzerland. **c.** Can modern man live without electricity? **d.** Mount Everest is much higher than Mont Blanc or the Matterhorn. **e.** I used to play the piano quite well, but now I'm completely out of practice. **f.** –. **g.** We hardly ever listen to the radio, but we often watch television. **h.** –. **i.** Don't most housewives go to town by bus? **j.** the.

---

5. Mit oder ohne a(n)?
a. He is always in a hurry. **b.** He smokes twenty cigarettes a day. **c.** I've got / I have some important information / an important piece of information for you. **d.** What colour would you like best? **e.** We sell a thousand bottles a month. **f.** Being an Englishwoman, she knows how to make good tea. **g.** What wonderful weather we're having! **h.** Why don't you read something for a change? **i.** If you have a temperature, you had better stay in bed. **j.** My brother-in-law, who is a lawyer, has given / gave me some good advice / a piece of good advice.

---

6. Steigerung und Vergleich
a. His daughter is just as unpleasant as he is. **b.** It isn't as easy / It is not

so easy as you may think. **c.** The station is even further / farther away than the airport. **d.** His eldest / (*U.S. auch:*) oldest son is two years older than I (am) / than me. **e.** The patient is getting / growing / becoming more and more restless. **f.** The quieter the hotel is, the better. **g.** He was more dead than alive when he arrived. **h.** This skyscraper is one of the tallest buildings in the world. **i.** He is one of the most intelligent people I know. **j.** You can pay the bill. You've got / You have the most money. **k.** The latest news is not very encouraging. **l.** Which is the shortest / quickest way to the town hall?

---

7. Mit oder ohne Stützwort?
a. The worst was yet to come. **b.** He is the best (man / boy) in the group. **c.** Who is going to look after / care for the sick? **d.** Children and sick people were evacuated first. **e.** The English have a long democratic tradition. **f.** He speaks English like an Englishman. **g.** There were also some English people / Englishmen staying at our hotel. **h.** Instead of buying a new machine, he had the old one repaired. **i.** This model is by far the best we can offer you. **j.** These tickets were rather expensive. I couldn't get any cheaper ones. **k.** German cameras are more expensive than Japanese ones.

---

8. Mit oder ohne -ly?
a. wise; unwisely. **b.** fresh; freshly. **c.** honest; certainly; honestly. **d.** pleasant; strangely sweet. **e.** dangerously near. **f.** usually; extremely fast. **g.** easy; easily. **h.** Admittedly; hard; hard. **i.** soundly; late; hardly; quickly. **j.** late lately. **k.** pretty cheaply. **l.** pretty; prettily.

---

9. Personalpronomen
a. He is stronger than me / than I (am). **b.** I didn't know (that) it was him. **c.** Somebody phoned. – Who was it? **d.** If it hadn't been for the dog, I would have (been) drowned. **e.** There aren't many foxes (a)round here. **f.** You / One can't do it like that. **g.** You / One can't help liking him. **h.** This expression can't be translated.

---

10. Possessivpronomen
a. He had a stick in his hand. **b.** Take your finger out of your nose! **c.** You must brush your teeth after each / every meal. **d.** He took her by the hand. **e.** He only kissed her on the shoulder. **f.** He wants to have a car of his own. **g.** This house isn't ours / doesn't belong to us. **h.** He is a good friend of mine. **i.** My photos aren't very good, but yours aren't any better.

---

11. Mit oder ohne -self / -selves?

a. Did / Have you hurt yourself? **b.** Did you apologize? / Have you apologized? **c.** We couldn't concentrate. **d.** We couldn't make ourselves understood. **e.** She turned round. **f.** She looked about her / looked round. **g.** They can't defend themselves. / You can't defend yourself / yourselves. **h.** They can't move. **i.** He complained to the manager. **j.** He introduced himself to the manager.

12. Interrogativpronomen

a. Who visited you, and who(m) did you visit? **b.** Who works for you, and who do you work for? **c.** Who gave you money, and who did you give money to? **d.** Who is this letter from? **e.** Who is this product distributed by? **f.** Who do these cows belong to? / Whose are these cows? **g.** Whose house will the meeting take place in / will the meeting be held in? **h.** What are you afraid of? **i.** What do these people live on? **j.** What are you going to specialize in? **k.** What is he complaining about? **l.** Which glass did you drink from / out of? **m.** Which Smith are you talking about? **n.** Which of you are / is going to the station?

13. Relativpronomen

a. who. **b.** that / which. **c.** –. **d.** The English, who have a long democratic tradition, don't use the word *democracy* very often. **e.** Henderson, whom many regard as one of our most capable politicians, will get an important cabinet post. **f.** that / which. **g.** –. **h.** whom. **i.** which. **j.** The victims, four of whom are in a critical condition, are all in St Mary's Hospital. **k.** Professor Smith, whose book on animal behaviour you may have read, has been awarded the Nobel Prize. **l.** They say that dogs that / which bark don't bite, but the dog that / which bit me apparently didn't know that saying.

14. Relativsätze ohne Relativpronomen

a. He ought to study something he is really interested in. **b.** The man the letter is addressed to has been dead for two years. **c.** He is constantly talking about things he knows nothing about. **d.** I am the only person he has confidence in. **e.** The hotel we stayed at last year has increased its prices by 30 per cent. **f.** The film the boy is looking at / watching is not really suitable for children. **g.** The matters they are now negotiating (about) are of the utmost importance. **h.** Luckily / Fortunately, the window he jumped from / out of was on the ground floor.

15. Präsens oder Perfekt?

a. I know him. I have known him for years. **b.** I am here. I have been here since two o'clock. **c.** We have / We've got a car. We have had this car for five years (now). **d.** It is raining. It has been raining since yesterday morning. **e.** Do you play chess? How long have you been playing chess? **f.** How long have you had this pain in your leg? **g.** We usually spend our holiday at the seaside. For years we have been spending our holidays at the seaside. **h.** Ever since that Alsatian bit me, I have been afraid of dogs.

16. Präteritum oder Perfekt?

a. Your parcel has arrived. **b.** Your parcel has just arrived. **c.** Your parcel arrived yesterday morning. **d.** Your parcel arrived this morning. **e.** Have you ever been to England? **f.** Weren't you in England last year? **g.** I was in England this summer. **h.** Have you seen / Did you see my new dress? **i.** Where did you last wear this dress? **j.** She has never worn this dress so far / up to now / yet. **k.** Where has he gone? **l.** He has already left. **m.** He left this afternoon. **n.** The train left a minute ago. **o.** The train has hardly ever been on time lately. **p.** Today the train was on time.

17. Einfache Form oder Verlaufsform?

a. you want; you're sitting. **b.** I'm not keeping. **c.** he plays. **d.** does; he always declares. **e.** is John doing. **f.** does John do. **g.** (being) serious. **h.** Did you mean. **i.** I've been meaning. **j.** have you been doing. **k.** read. **l.** be sitting. **m.** were having; came; were having; left; be eating. **n.** been snowing.

18. Zukunft

a. This is the quietest room I can offer you. – All right, I'll take it. **b.** I'll probably see you in the morning, then. **c.** Will we be allowed to use the swimming pool? **d.** When you read these lines, I'll be dead. **e.** I won't / shan't be long. **f.** From now on I'll tell / I'm going to tell the truth. **g.** Are you going to accept the offer? **h.** I (can) feel something is going to happen. **i.** How long are you going to stay / will you be staying? **j.** We're going swimming / for a swim. Are you coming (with us)? **k.** The washing machine is being delivered tomorrow afternoon. **l.** We're giving / throwing a party on Saturday. **m.** We're / We'll be watching television tonight / this evening. **n.** Who will be / is conducting today's / tonight's concert? **o.** I'm / I'll be leaving the day after tomorrow. **p.** I'm sure / I imagine you'll be celebrating tonight. **q.** He starts work tomorrow morning. **r.** Don't forget (that) the Chancellor expects you this afternoon.   **s.** I hope you / you'll enjoy the performance.

19. Bedingungssätze I
a. would go. **b.** is. **c.** had been. **d.** would be. **e.** tell. **f.** would be. **g.** had been. **h.** would never read. **i.** would not have invented.

20. Bedingungssätze II
a. If I wasn't / weren't so tired, I'd / I would work in the garden a bit / for a while. **b.** If I were you, I wouldn't go by car. **c.** If we had two keys, you could have one too. **d.** We'd / We would probably have had less trouble if we had bought the more expensive model. **e.** The game / match would have been more fun if it had not been raining all the time. **f.** If we had stayed at home, we would have saved a lot of time and petrol / (*U.S.:*) gas. **g.** If we had caught the earlier train, we would have arrived on time / punctually. **h.** If it wasn't / weren't for the dog, we would rent a flat / (*U.S.:*) apartment in the city centre. **i.** If it hadn't been for the dog, we would have travelled by train.

21. Indirekte Rede und Frage
a. They promised (that) there wouldn't be any further delays. **b.** He told me (that) that could be arranged. **c.** They informed us that they didn't have any plastic ones. **d.** The reviewer wrote (that) there was nothing wrong with the book except that it was unreadable. **e.** They told me (that) they would have to test me first. **f.** He insisted that there must be a leak somewhere. **g.** He claimed (that) he had noticed nothing unusual. **h.** George Orwell once remarked that the Swiss had managed to build a lovely country around their hotels. **i.** She asked if she might come tomorrow / the next day. **j.** Clemenceau once said that everything he knew he had learnt after he was thirty. **k.** She asked me if I had known him long. **l.** He asked me when I expected to be back. **m.** Everybody was wondering where she had gone. **n.** Nobody knew how he had managed to get a permit. **o.** He says (that) the cheque hasn't arrived yet. **p.** The firm claims that the material is absolutely waterproof. **q.** He reminded us of the eternal truth that a rich man's joke is always funny. **r.** I think it was Disraeli who observed that it is much easier to be critical than to be correct.

22. Passiv I
a. The windows are cleaned once a month. **b.** A black umbrella was found near the (dead) body. **c.** The school was founded by monks in the fifteenth century. **d.** Have the beds been made? **e.** Never before had the competi-

tion / contest been won by a woman. **f.** This problem could easily be solved. **g.** Part of the stomach had to be removed. **h.** He will probably have to be operated on. **i.** The patient is being examined (right) now. / The patient is just being examined (now). **j.** He suspected that he was still being shadowed. **k.** Who were these photos taken by?

---

23. Passiv II
a. He wasn't allowed to go swimming. **b.** I was assured that the matter would be investigated. **c.** They can't be expected to be helpful in any way. **d.** The old man had to be helped up to the platform. **e.** We were joined by a large number of volunteers. **f.** She was shown how to operate the machine. **g.** Who will he be succeeded by? **h.** They were told to be quiet. **i.** Can she be trusted?

---

24. Passiv III
a. I was asked some questions. **b.** She was given a letter to translate. **c.** He was handed a bunch of flowers. **d.** We were offered a table by the window. **e.** They were paid a satisfactory price. **f.** Were you promised a reward? **g.** I was shown some interesting new models. **h.** I hope he'll be taught a lesson.

---

25. Infinitiv nach Fragewörtern und whether
a. I had no idea what to say. **b.** Do you know how to get there? **c.** He knows how to handle horses. **d.** She didn't know whether to laugh or cry. **e.** She knows when to leave her husband alone. **f.** We don't know who(m) to invite to our wedding. **g.** I'm thinking about which tie to put on. **h.** They quarrelled over where to spend their holiday.

---

26. Infinitiv in relativsatzähnlicher Funktion
a. I was one of the last to see him alive. **b.** I would have been the first to admit that. **c.** There's nothing to indicate that the murderer is left-handed. **d.** He chose five men to accompany him on his expedition. **e.** There's a Mr Butler to see you(, sir). **f.** She takes an interest in / She is interested in everything to do with his work. **g.** I'll give you a book to read on / in the plane. **h.** I need someone / somebody to talk to. **i.** She didn't see anything to laugh about. **j.** She didn't suffer; that's something to be grateful / thankful for.

---

27. Infinitiv und -ing-Form nach Substantiven
a. to persuade. **b.** to conceal. **c.** of overworking. **d.** in torturing. **e.** not to give up. **f.** in finding. **g.** in / of changing. **h.** to criticize. **i.** to discuss.

j. of discussing. **k.** of getting. **l.** of being. **m.** to survive. **n.** of doing. **o.** to retire. **p.** of learning. **q.** to accept. **r.** to leave. **s.** for discussing / to discuss. **t.** in continuing. **u.** to do. **v.** of welcoming. **w.** for wanting. **x.** of being. **y.** to reject or shorten. **z.** of sending.

28. Infinitiv und -ing-Form nach Verben

a. (to) being. **b.** beginning. **c.** to buy. **d.** in collecting. **e.** to continue. **f.** in giving. **g.** being. **h.** to know. **i.** of being. **j.** joining. **k.** starting. **l.** to start looking. **m.** in going. **n.** being. **o.** being. **p.** watering. **q.** being. **r.** repairing. **s.** regarding. **t.** to make. **u.** interrupting. **v.** to paying. **w.** in calling. **x.** not going. **y.** to use. **z.** in being.

29. Objekt-Infinitiv-Konstruktion

a. Allow me to introduce myself. **b.** I don't know what caused / induced him to postpone his decision. **c.** We couldn't get / persuade him to put a coat on. **d.** I hate anyone / anybody to watch me working. **e.** I love you to read me stories in the evening. **f.** The officer ordered his men not to shoot. **g.** I'd / I would / I should prefer you to play something by Mozart. **h.** Please remind me to buy the theatre tickets. **i.** She told me to remind you of the presents. **j.** I trust you to do it tactfully. **k.** Why don't you want the dog to sleep on the sofa?

30. Passiv der Objekt-Infinitiv-Konstruktion

a. He was advised to go to the Central Library. **b.** I was asked to sign the document. **c.** Who will be chosen to represent us at the conference? **d.** The project is expected to move slowly. **e.** They were forced to shut down their factory. **f.** I was hired to do all the dirty work. **g.** Can you be persuaded to come with us? **h.** She was told not to open the door. **i.** The children must be warned not to touch the wires. **j.** He was never heard to speak kindly to his wife. **k.** He was seen to walk down the High Street. **l.** The prisoners were made to march to the station. **m.** All foreigners should be made to feel at home.

31. Aktiver oder passiver Infinitiv?

a. be foreseen. **b.** foresee. **c.** do. **d.** be done. **e.** talk. **f.** seek. **g.** be seen. **h.** be done. **i.** be parked. **j.** take. **k.** see. **l.** be taken. **m.** believe. **n.** confuse. **o.** produce. **p.** be opened. **q.** live / be lived. **r.** be answered.

32. -ing-Konstruktion mit eigenem Sinnsubjekt

a. You don't mind me / my calling you Piggy? **b.** I remember you / your mentioning his name. **c.** I can't imagine him / his ever being afraid.

d. Everything now depends on her being at home / (*U.S.:*) being home. **e.** There's no sense in us / our quarrelling. **f.** How did you manage to carry them upstairs without them / their waking up? **g.** I'm sick of everybody / everyone asking me that question. **h.** I'm surprised at a man like you paying attention to rumours.

---

33. -ing-Konstruktion in relativsatzähnlicher Funktion

a. Is there a bus going up to the castle? **b.** Inside every fat man is a thin one wanting to get out. **c.** The road connecting the two villages is very narrow. **d.** The people doing this work are paid extremely well. **e.** The money lying on the table is for you. **f.** For everyone / everybody wishing to learn English this is the quickest way to success. **g.** Are you sure there are no other documents lying about somewhere? **h.** The people living here are all friendly and helpful. **i.** The bomb killed a policeman standing nearby. **j.** The prints hanging on the wall are all by the same artist.

---

34. -ing-Konstruktion als adverbiale Bestimmung

a. Putting down the newspaper / Putting the newspaper down, she went into / in the kitchen. **b.** Taking her in his arms, he kissed her. **c.** Opening her handbag, she took out a packet of cigarettes. **d.** He was standing in front of the mirror, shaving with an electric razor. **e.** She cut her hand while washing up. **f.** Having locked / After locking / Locking the door carefully, she put on the lights and opened the window. **g.** Being both clever and patient, he was a dangerous opponent. **h.** Being unable to drive a car, he always goes by taxi. **i.** Seeing that the boy's feet were wet, she lit a fire and took off his shoes / took his shoes off. **j.** Being very hungry, I didn't mind what I was eating.

---

35. Partizip Perfekt

a. The statistics contained in the book are completely out of date. **b.** Some of the proposals / suggestions made by him are quite reasonable. **c.** The work done by the committee / commission is of great value to all of us / to us all. **d.** The conversation mentioned by you did not take place on the twenty-third. **e.** Policemen armed with machine guns were to be seen everywhere. **f.** None of the arguments put forward was very convincing. **g.** The new models shown at the exhibition are very interesting. **h.** England and America are two countries separated by the same language. **i.** (Having) Arrived in Camford, they drove straight to the hospital. **j.** Though praised by the critics, the book never became a best seller. **k.** Though officially invited, he didn't attend the meeting.

---

36. Verben mit zwei Objekten

a. She showed me the letter. **b.** She showed the letter to all sorts of people. **c.** She showed me a carbon (copy) / a copy of the letter she had written (to) him. **d.** She showed it (to) me. / She showed me it. **e.** She showed it to her lawyer. **f.** Who did she show the letter to? **g.** Who did she show it to? **h.** The letter was shown to her lawyer. **i.** Why wasn't he sent a copy of the letter? / Why wasn't a copy of the letter sent to him / (*U.S.:*) sent him? **j.** Who was the letter shown to? **k.** Can you explain that to me? **l.** Can I dictate some more letters to you? **m.** I wouldn't have found the house if you hadn't described it to me. **n.** I envy you your wonderful / marvellous voice.

37. Stellung des Objekts bei Phrasal Verbs

a. When did you send the letter off? **b.** I('ve) sent off the letter / sent the letter off but not the parcel. **c.** Have you sent it off? **d.** Don't forget to turn the water off / to turn off the water. **e.** Drink your beer up! / Drink up your beer! **f.** We've drunk up all the beer in the house. **g.** Did you fill in / Have you filled in the forms I gave you yesterday? **h.** If you lend him money, you'll never get it back. **i.** I must try to get back the money I lent him. **j.** The room will look nicer / prettier when I've hung up all the pictures / hung all the pictures up. **k.** When are you going to hang them up?

38. Prädikative Ergänzung zum Objekt

a. An extremist doesn't have a chance / has no chance / hasn't a chance of being elected President. **b.** He hopes to be elected President. **c.** The President made him his closest adviser. **d.** He was made a hero against his will. **e.** He has been appointed ambassador to Switzerland. **f.** They proclaimed / declared the first of May a national holiday. / The first of May was proclaimed / declared a national holiday. **g.** I have always considered you my friend / regarded you as my friend. **h.** This is generally considered the best / regarded as the best solution.

39. Mit oder ohne do-Umschreibung?

a. Do you want to see him? Can you see him? **b.** Who gave him money? Who did he give money to? **c.** We didn't want to invite him. We couldn't invite him. **d.** He hates not being / not to be consulted. He doesn't like being / to be disturbed. **e.** He invited not only his colleagues but also all his students. **f.** Is it slippery outside? – I hope not. **g.** Don't get excited / upset! / Don't upset yourself! Don't be too generous! **h.** I needn't help you, need I? / I don't need to help you, do I? I don't need a visa, do I?

i. Don't you often invite people to / for lunch / dinner? Don't you often have guests (in)? Haven't you informed him?

---

40. Have mit oder ohne do-Umschreibung?
a. Do we have / Have we got any milk in the house? **b.** Did he have a bath last night? **c.** We haven't got / haven't caught / don't have the murderer yet. **d.** Do you have / Have you (got) any brothers and sisters? **e.** When do you usually / normally have breakfast? **f.** Do you have many thefts? **g.** Don't you have / Haven't you (got) any pride? **h.** Don't you usually / normally have a cold at this time of (the) year? **i.** How many young do these animals normally / usually / generally have? **j.** Why didn't you have a swimming pool built in the garden?

---

41. Hilfsverben in Kurzantworten
a. Do you like this kind / sort of music? – Yes, I do. / No, I don't. **b.** Can she swim? – Yes, she can. / No, she can't. **c.** I enjoy this music very much. – So do I. **d.** I could do with a Scotch now. – So could I. **e.** I can't stand him. – Nor / Neither can I. **f.** We never watch TV / television / (the) telly. – Nor / Neither do we. **g.** I love you, Brigitte. – I love you too, George. **h.** Who could (go to) meet the boy at the airport? – Aunt Alice could. **i.** I don't mind mice. – But I do! **j.** Why didn't you inform him / let him know? – But I did!

---

42. Hilfsverben in Frageanhängseln
a. won't he. **b.** didn't I. **c.** hasn't he. **d.** isn't it. **e.** isn't it. **f.** hasn't it. **g.** aren't I. **h.** didn't she / use(d)n't she. **i.** oughtn't he. **j.** do you. **k.** should I. **l.** do we. **m.** can you. **n.** am I. **o.** does she. **p.** did you. **q.** is there. **r.** will we / shall we. **s.** have you. **t.** shall we. **u.** shall we. **v.** won't you / will you.

---

43. Fragekonstruktion in Nichtfragesätzen (Inversion)
a. Hardly had they shaken hands when they started quarrelling. **b.** Hardly had we arrived at the theatre when I realized I'd left the tickets at home. **c.** Scarcely had you left when the trouble started. **d.** No sooner had the shooting begun than Busty fell flat on his face with remarkable speed. **e.** No sooner did Mr Davies get home than he had a very bad pain in his chest. **f.** Never did the parents interfere in their son's affairs. **g.** Rarely have I met such generous people. **h.** Only now did he become conscious of all that he had forgotten. **i.** Only if you're moving can they see you. **j.** In vain did he try to get his neighbours to help him.

44. Konjunktionen
a. After our guests had left, we drank / had another bottle of wine. **b.** The boy is growing / becoming more and more sensible. **c.** As / Since you don't like the Browns, we won't / shan't invite them. **d.** You talk as if / as though you were my father. **e.** You can watch that silly TV show as long as / so long as you don't expect me to watch it too. **f.** We'll tackle / attack this problem as soon as we come / get back. **g.** By the time we go on holiday, the operation will be forgotten. **h.** We'll build the house even if the situation gets worse / changes for the worse. **i.** I doubt if / whether that's the whole truth. **j.** Take a road map with you / (*U.S.:*) along (just) in case you lose your way. **k.** Once you are back at home, you can listen to all these records. **l.** Supposing we win a million on the football pools, would that be enough to pay our debts? **m.** I won't / shan't be able to pay the rent until next week. **n.** Whenever I am in London, I go to a Chinese restaurant in Gerrard Street. **o.** He came while we were out.

45. Präpositionen I
a. How much money do you have in your bank account at the moment? **b.** on. **c.** to. **d.** Why don't you apply for a position in the export department? **e.** –. **f.** Since you've been in hospital she's asked / inquired after / about you every day. **g.** in. **h.** for. **i.** for. **j.** for. **k.** at. **l.** on. **m.** to. **n.** on / (*U.S. auch:*) for. **o.** of. **p.** in. **q.** with. **r.** of. **s.** from. **t.** in. **u.** with. **v.** to. **w.** to. **x.** –. **y.** at. **z.** They didn't go out for fear of being seen.

46. Präpositionen II
a. of. **b.** for. **c.** with. **d.** of. **e.** in / for. **f.** for. **g.** on. **h.** I've been looking for my gloves for half an hour, but I can't find them. **i.** by. **j.** by. **k.** with. **l.** by. **m.** She had to be operated on for cancer. **n.** Athletes from fifteen nations took part in the race. **o.** They paid for the latest shipment by cheque. **p.** –. **q.** In. **r.** She takes great pride in her dog's ability to stand on his hind legs, but I'm sure that's nothing out of the ordinary. **s.** on. **t.** With / (*U.S.:*) In regard to your application for credit we are still waiting for instructions from Head Office. **u.** with / by. **v.** for. **w.** of. **x.** in. **y.** at. **z.** from.

47. Präpositionen III
a. at / on. **b.** above / beyond. **c.** of. **d.** on. **e.** on. **f.** on. **g.** Are you going there by train or by car? **h.** with. **i.** This way of dealing with the crisis is typical of the President. **j.** of. **k.** In view of the economic situation our plans for expansion may have to be reconsidered. **l.** Our general manager

has just left for a visit to our Dublin branch. **m.** in. **n.** for. **o.** on. **p.** to.
q. –. **r.** On. **s.** in.

---

48. Unregelmäßige Verben

a. This problem first arose towards / (*U.S.:*) toward the end of the war.
b. Some serious difficulties have arisen. **c.** She had borne him five sons.
The last one was born on March 8, 1812. **d.** So far / Up to now / Up till
now he has never beaten me at chess. **e.** The book was bound in leather.
f. Has the dog ever bitten you? – Yes, he sometimes bit me when he was
young. **g.** Someone / Somebody must have blown out the candles. **h.** You
might / could easily have broken your neck! **i.** The programme was broadcast last Friday / on Friday last. **j.** The police have caught the kidnappers.
k. The ring she chose cost a small fortune. **l.** In his latest book he has dealt
with this problem at length / in detail. **m.** I ate too much during the holidays. **n.** I have never felt better than now / than at present. **o.** He (has)
fought on many fronts. **p.** When he flew to Munich yesterday, he behaved
as if / as though he had never flown before. **q.** I've hung up my coat. **r.** In
the Middle Ages thieves were frequently hanged. **s.** Here's the five pounds
you lent me last Sunday. **t.** The cost of living rose considerably last year.
u. I set my watch by the station clock this morning. **v.** The rumour spread
quickly. **w.** The clock has just struck. **x.** Be careful, I've just swept the
floor. **y.** In 1940 a thirty-year-old American butcher swam 292 miles in
89 hours (and) 48 minutes. **z.** I woke up at five o'clock this morning.
I wish I hadn't woken up so early.

---

49. "Dürfen"

a. May I remind you of your promise? **b.** May I interrupt you for a moment? – No, you may not. **c.** I mustn't smoke so much. **d.** You mustn't
always make promises you can't keep. **e.** Why wasn't he allowed to stay
longer? **f.** Will we be allowed to use the large hall? **g.** We hope to be
allowed to use the large hall. **h.** So far, she hasn't been allowed to visit
him. **i.** This kind of machine ought to / should be easy to install / set up.
j. You shouldn't have given up so quickly / soon.

---

50. "Können"

a. Can you play something by Brahms? **b.** Can you speak / Do you know
French? **c.** Can't the machine be repaired? **d.** He can't have dug the hole
himself. **e.** She couldn't lift / She was unable to lift the stone off the ground.
f. They were able to sell the house at a reasonable price. **g.** Couldn't we
go by train too? **h.** I could swim when I was only five. **i.** We could also
get along / manage / cope without oil. / We could get along / manage with-

out oil too / as well. **j.** She said she couldn't help me. **k.** This could be my umbrella. **l.** The train may have been late. **m.** The train may not be on time. **n.** The train might / could have been late. **o.** I couldn't have killed the rabbit. **p.** He thought the tablets might help. **q.** We won't / shan't be able to go by car. **r.** He seems to be unable / He doesn't seem (to be) able to translate the text.

51. "Lassen"

a. You can leave your coat here. **b.** Why do you always leave the door open? **c.** Leave the dog alone / in peace! **d.** He wanted to make a speech, but they didn't / wouldn't let him. **e.** She won't let the boy go. / She won't allow the boy to go. **f.** The teacher had us / made us learn the poem by heart. / The teacher got / told us to learn the poem by heart. **g.** She had the window frames painted green. **h.** We'll have to have / We'll have to get the dog vaccinated. **i.** We try not to keep our patients waiting too long. **j.** If it doesn't get better / improve, we'll have to send for the doctor.

52. "Machen"

a. You could at least try to make a good impression. **b.** Please make yourself / yourselves comfortable! **c.** I've just had a new suit made. **d.** She has made him a happy man. **e.** I haven't made / done the beds yet. **f.** When are you going to do the bedroom? **g.** If you want to do business with the people here, you must be patient. / If one wants to do business with the people here, one must be patient. **h.** I don't know what to do. **i.** Has the boy done his homework / his prep? **j.** How is your father doing? **k.** She goes for / takes a long walk every morning. **l.** The pain is driving me mad / crazy. **m.** That doesn't matter! **n.** It's time I got to work. **o.** Three bottles at 70 pence each – that's two pounds ten (pence / p).

53. "Müssen"

a. I / I've had to do it. **b.** He must have done it. **c.** I have to / must be at the office at half past seven every morning. **d.** I have to go / I've got to go / I must go to the doctor('s) tomorrow morning. **e.** It must have been raining. **f.** We must all do our duty. **g.** We have to / must change at Crewe. **h.** You mustn't be so rude to him all the time. **i.** You can attend the service, but you don't have to. **j.** I'm afraid I'll have to go now. **k.** She'll have to stay in hospital for at least another two weeks / another fortnight. **l.** He had to be operated on immediately / at once. **m.** He ought to have known that.

54. "Sollen"

a. You're to phone him at once / immediately / right away. **b.** The boss is not to be / doesn't want to be disturbed. **c.** We were never to see him again. **d.** What's that supposed to mean? **e.** This drawing is said / is supposed to be by Picasso. **f.** Next winter is expected to be very cold. **g.** The hotel is said / is supposed to be one of the most expensive on the south coast. **h.** Shall I put / Do you want me to put the tins / (*U.S.:*) cans in the fridge / refrigerator / (*U.S. auch:*) icebox? **i.** This must not / shall not happen again! **j.** One should never promise too much. **k.** (Actually,) The boots should be / ought to be / are supposed to be watertight. **l.** If anything should happen, please ring / phone me immediately. **m.** She told me to wait / She said I should wait for her here. **n.** We should have / ought to have consulted an expert. **o.** You shouldn't have left / oughtn't to have left the windows open.

55. "Werden"

a. I hope you / you'll get well / better soon. **b.** I got so tired during the speech that I couldn't keep my eyes open. **c.** It was just getting / turning dark when / as we arrived. **d.** If my secretary is taken ill / falls ill, I'll be in an awful fix. / (*U.S.:*) If my secretary gets / falls / takes sick, I'll be in an awful fix. **e.** It's going to be hot today. **f.** His eldest / oldest son is probably going to be a musician. **g.** His eldest / oldest son has become a musician. **h.** What will become of the dog when / if the old woman dies? **i.** His hair has turned white overnight. **j.** My coffee has gone cold. **k.** I'd go crazy / mad if I had to work here. **l.** The days are growing shorter / longer.

56. "All", "ganz", "jeder", "kein"

a. All for one, one for all. **b.** All the lights / lamps were on. **c.** Everybody / Everyone knew where he was hiding. / They all knew where he was hiding. **d.** He gets an injection / a shot every two hours. **e.** He really seems to know everything. **f.** Life here is anything but pleasant. **g.** Please tell the truth – the whole truth, and nothing but the truth! **h.** She left all (of) her money / the whole of her money to the London Zoo. **i.** He's quite a different / a completely different person when his wife isn't with him. **j.** On the whole our situation isn't (any) worse than (it was) last year. **k.** The whole thing was a bluff. **l.** Everybody / Everyone knew what (he had) to do. **m.** Each of them / Every one of them knew what was at stake. **n.** Every housewife needs Persil. **o.** You can phone / ring / call me (at) any time. **p.** Anybody / Anyone can say that! **q.** Unfortunately we didn't have any / had no money at all. **r.** I don't need any advice from you. **s.** Nobody /

No one knows what he meant by that. **t.** None of us had an answer to that question. **u.** Neither of the two proposals / suggestions seems to be acceptable. **v.** I wouldn't invite either of them.

57. "Sehr"

a. She's a very attractive girl. He loves her very much. They're very much in love. **b.** He may come by the next train, but I doubt it very much. The outcome of the election is still very much in doubt. The future looks very doubtful. **c.** He was very interested / very much interested in the story. The story interested him very much. He found the story very interesting. **d.** We'd like very much to see the film. We're very anxious to get tickets for the show. **e.** He is (very) much respected by all his neighbours. He is a much respected member of the community. **f.** (very) much.

58. Some – any

a. Won't you have some tea? – No, thanks, I couldn't drink anything at the moment, but I'll have some tea later if you don't mind. **b.** Would you like anything / something to eat? – No, thank you, I had something on the train. **c.** Can I offer you something / anything? – Yes, do you happen to have any / some whisky in the house? Scotch is something I really care for after a long walk. **d.** I don't think there's anything to worry about at this point. But if you have any difficulty, let me know. **e.** I can't see anybody laughing. Did I say something serious for a change? **f.** You look upset. Is something / anything wrong? Did I do something you didn't like? Why don't you say something / anything? **g.** Isn't there anything else you can do besides read the damn newspapers all day? Don't you have any hobbies? You can do anything you like, but don't just sit there reading the News of the World! **h.** You can come any time you like, but do bring something to write. **i.** We may regret this decision some day, but for the time being any decision is better than no decision at all.

59. Zahlen

a. a half / one half, two and a half; five and a third, two thirds; a quarter / one quarter, seven and three quarters, five fourths; a fifth / one fifth, two fifths, three fifths; nine and one / a sixth, four sixths, three and five sixths. **b.** one fiftieth, two over twenty-five / two twenty-fifths; eighty-five over two hundred and fifty, a / one hundred and ninety-three over four hundred and seventy-seven / (*U.S. auch:*) a / one hundred ninety-three over four hundred seventy-seven. **c.** ten point five six three, ten thousand five hundred and sixty-three / (*U.S. auch:*) ten thousand five hundred sixty-three; seven point eight five, seven thousand eight hundred and fifty / (*U.S. auch:*) seven thousand eight hundred fifty.

d. four, fourteen, forty; five, fifteen, fifty; eight, eighteen, eighty.

e. a / one hundred, a / one hundred and six / (*U.S. auch:*) a / one hundred six, a / one hundred and sixteen / (*U.S. auch:*) a / one hundred sixteen, a / one hundred and twenty-seven / (*U.S. auch:*) a / one hundred twenty-seven.

f. one thousand two hundred and thirty-six / (*U.S. auch:*) one thousand two hundred thirty-six, one thousand three hundred and seventy-nine / (*U.S. auch:*) one thousand three hundred seventy-nine; five thousand nine hundred and seventy-eight / (*U.S. auch:*) five thousand nine hundred seventy-eight, twenty-four thousand nine hundred and thirty-two / (*U.S. auch:*) twenty-four thousand nine hundred thirty-two, a / one hundred thousand, a / one million.

g. ten sixty-six, fifteen hundred and twelve / fifteen twelve, eighteen hundred and ten / eighteen ten, nineteen seventy-four / nineteen hundred and seventy-four.

h. six oh six three oh three oh, three seven oh four nine double three, two three five seven oh four oh; five eight one eight one double oh, six double seven three one double oh, double eight nine four three one oh. (Im U.S.-Englisch statt *oh* manchmal auch *zero*.)

---

60. Datum

a. January (the) first, nineteen seventy-four
July (the) twenty-seventh, nineteen fifty-five

b. the second (of) February nineteen thirty-six
the twenty-eighth (of) August, eighteen ninety-nine

c. March (the) third, nineteen-sixty
September (the) twenty-ninth, two thousand

d. the fourth (of) April, nineteen hundred
the thirtieth (of) October nineteen eighty

e. the twenty-fifth (of) May, nineteen seventy-three
the twenty-second (of) November, nineteen seventy-two

f. June (the) twenty-first, nineteen seventy
December (the) twenty-third, nineteen forty-nine

(In förmlichem Stil jeweils auch *nineteen hundred and seventy-four, nineteen hundred and fifty-five* usw.)

WORTSCHATZREGISTER ENGLISCH

Die Zahlen bezeichnen die Seiten, auf denen die Wörter in den englisch-deutschen Vokabelerklärungen vorkommen.

absolutely 27
accept 24
acceptable 62
accident 19
accompany 32
ache 7
act 14
address 20
admit 14, 32
advance 29
advice 8, 10
advise 29, 36
adviser 44
affair 49
afford 10
afraid 18, 21, 38
after-shave lotion 14
afternoon 22
against 44
airport 12, 47
alive 12, 32
along 50, 56
Alsatian 21
always 40
ambassador 44
animal 46
another 50
anxious 63
apparently 19
appoint 44
argument 41
armed 41
arrive 26
artist 39
ask 30, 38
assure 29
attack 50
attend 41, 59
attention 38
attractive 63

automobile 25
awake 38
award 19
away 61
awful 61

back 7, 43
bad 49
badly 17
bath 46
become 49
bed 28
bedroom 58
beef 60
beer 43
behave 48
belong 18
bill 12
billiards 48
birthday present 35
bit 19, 21
bite 19, 21
bitten 19, 21
blue whale 53
bluff 62
body 28
bomb 39
book 29
boots 60
bored 48
both . . . and 40
bottle 11, 50, 58
boy 50
branch 53
breakfast 46
brother 46
brother-in-law 11
brush 7
building 12
bunch 30

bury 12, 23
bus 39
business 25
by far 13
by heart 57

cake 14
call 38, 62
camera 13
cancer 32
capable 19
car 26, 40, 56
carbon (copy) 42
care 64
carefully 40
case 8, 9
castle 39
catch 7, 26
caught 7, 26
cause 35
celebrate 24
centre 26
century 28
certain 14
chair 58
change 11, 59, 64
chess 21, 48
chest 49
children 20
Chinese 50
choose 32
chose 32
chosen 32
cigarette 11, 40
city centre 26
claim 27
clean 28
clever 40
close 44
coat 35, 57

rabbit 56
rather 8
razor 40
read 35
realize 49
really 20
reasonable 41, 56
reconsider 53
record 50
refrigerator 60
regard 19
regret 64
relax 37
remarkable 49
remember 25, 38
remind 35, 55
remove 28
rent 26, 50
repair 13, 56
represent 36
respect 63
restaurant 50
restless 12
reviewer 27
reward 30
rice 18
ring 62
road 36, 39, 45
road map 50
Roman 25
room 12, 24, 38
round 17
rude 59
rumour 38

satisfactory 30
satisfied 53
sauce 14
save 26
saying 19
scarcely 49
school 28
Scotch 47
seaside 21
seek 37
send off 43

sensible 50
separate 41
seriously 37
service 59
set out 49
severe 32
shadow 28
shave 40
shoot 35
shot 35
shoulder 16
show 50
shut down 36
sick 38
sign 36
silly 50
simple 12
sing 64
sister 46
situation 50
size 38
skyscraper 12
slippery 45
smoke 11, 38
so far 55
sofa 35
solution 44
solve 28
somehow 38
son 61
song 64
soon 49, 57
sort 42
sought 37
spare parts 19
speak 14
specialize 18
speech 57
speed 49
spend 21, 31
spoke 14
stain 28
stake 62
stand 39, 47
start 24
station 18

statistics 41
stay 10, 11, 13, 20, 29, 36, 38, 59
stay away 61
steep 8
stick 16
stomach 28
stone 17, 56
story 35
strange 14
student 45
succeed 29
success 39
suffer 9, 32
suit 58
suitable 20
suitcase 18
supper 23
supply 19
surprised 38
suspect 28
swimming pool 24, 46
Switzerland 44
symptom 32

table 30
tablet 56
tackle 50
tactful(ly) 35
take 16, 28, 56
take along 50
take place 18, 41
talk 18, 32
tall 12
task 12
taste 14
taxi 40
teach 30
technical term 19
teeth 16
television 24, 47
tell 24, 25
temper 14
term 19
text 56
theatre 13

theatre tickets 35
theft 46
think about 31
this afternoon 22
this morning 14, 22
threat 37
thriller 53
ticket 7, 13, 35, 63
tie 31
time 22, 26
time of (the) year 46
timid 53
tin 60
tired 26
tomorrow morning 59
tooth 16
top 24
touch 36
town centre 26
town hall 12
tradition 13
traffic accident 19
train 22, 26, 56
translate 15, 30, 56
travel 26
trouble 26
true 24, 63
trust 29, 35
truth 14, 24, 25
turn 7
turn off 43

turn round 17
TV show 50

umbrella 28
unpleasant 12
unwise 14
upset 45, 64
upstairs 38
use 63
used to 10
usually 10, 46
utmost 20

vaccinate 57
vain 49
valuable 39
victim 19
victory 24
village 39
visa 45
visit 18
voice 42
volunteer 29

wait 60
wake up 38
walk 16, 58
wall 39
want 23, 39
wash up 40
washing machine 24

watch 35, 50
watch television 24, 47
waterproof 27
watertight 60
way 50
wear 22
weather 11, 38
wedding 31
whale 53
whisky 11
will 44
win 28, 50
window 20, 28, 30, 60
window frame 57
wine 50, 64
wire 36
woke(n) up 38
wonder 27
wonderful 11, 42
wore 22
work 35, 38
world 25
worn 22
worse 50
wound 46

year 63
yesterday 22
young 46

zoo 62

WORTSCHATZREGISTER DEUTSCH

Die Zahlen bezeichnen die Seiten, auf denen die Wörter in den englisch-deutschen Vokabelerklärungen vorkommen.

Gebäude 12
geben 25
Gebrauch 63
Geburtstagsgeschenk 35
Gedicht 57
Geduld 14, 58
geduldig 40
geeignet 20
gefährlich 40
gefallen 47
Gefangene(r) 36
gegen 44
Gegner 40
gehen 16, 18
gehören 18
Geld 43, 63
Gemeinschaft 63
gemütlich 53
Genehmigung 27
Generaldirektor 53
gerade erst 49
gern haben 15
Gerücht 38
Geschäftsführer 17
Geschichte 20, 32, 35
geschickt 40
Geschmack 14
Geschwister 46
Gespräch 41
gestern früh 22
gewaltig 10
gewinnen 28, 50
gewiß 14
glatt 45
glücklich 58
glücklicherweise 20
Gottesdienst 59
graben 56
Gras 7
gratulieren 37
grob 59
groß 55, 58
Größe 38
großzügig 45, 49
gründen 28
Gruppe 29

Haare 7
Häftling 36
halten 7, 55, 57
halten für 19, 44
Hand 40
handeln 14
Handtasche 40
hauptsächlich 18
Haus 37
Hausarbeiten 58
Hausaufgaben 58
Hausfrau 10, 62
heben 56
heiraten 23
heißen 60
Held 44
helfen 49
herauswollen 39
herrlich 11
heute morgen 14, 22
heute nachmittag 22
hierherkommen 31
hilfsbereit 29, 39
hinaus 39
hindeuten auf 32
hinlegen 40
hoch 12
Hochzeit 31
Hoffnung 55
Hotel 10, 13, 20
hübsch 43
Hund 15, 18, 21, 38

ignorieren 10
im allgemeinen 46
im voraus 29
impfen 57
Information 11, 45
Ingenieur 23
Inhalt 8
insgesamt 7
installieren 55
Interesse an 63
interessieren 20, 32
interessiert an 63

irgendwie 38
Italien 31

Jahr 63
Jahreszeit 46
Jahrhundert 28
je 58
jedermann 63
Junge 46, 50

kalt werden 48
Kamera 13
Kaninchen 56
Karte 7, 13, 63
kaum . . . als 49
kennen 19, 48
Kerl 59
Kinder 20
Kiste 8
klar werden 49
Klavier 10
Kleid 8, 22
klein 31
Knoblauch 14
Koffer 18
Kollege 45
Kollegin 45
Komitee 41
Konferenz 36
konzentrieren 17
Konzert 24
Kopie 42
Kosten 9
Krankenhaus 59
Krankheit 9
kriegen 26
Krimi 53
Krise 9
Kritiker(in) 27, 41
Kuchen 14
Kühlschrank 60
kümmern 13, 25
Künstler(in) 39
Kursteilnehmer(in) 45
kurz 7

Laie 37
lang 58
Langstreckenflug 7
langweilen 48
Lärm 18
lassen 31
Latein 25
Lateinisch 25
Leben 10
leben 18
lebend 32
lebendig 12, 32
Leck 27
Leiche 28
Leichnam 28
leid sein 38
leiden 9, 32
leihen 43
leisten 10
Leitung 36
Lektion 30
lernen 25, 57
letzte 22, 23, 63
Leute 42
Licht machen 40
Lieblingsfarbe 11
Lied 64
liefern 8, 24
Linkshänder 32
loben 9, 41
Loch 27
lösen 28
Lösung 44
Lungenkrebs 32

machen 16, 20, 26, 28,
  40, 55, 64
Mädchen 31, 63
Magen 28
Mahlzeit 16
Mantel 35, 57
Maschine 13, 29, 55, 56
Maschinengewehr 41
Maus 47
Mäuse 47
meistens 10

Menge 62
Mensch 58
merken 25
Miete 50
mieten 26
Million 50
miserabel 48
mit Abstand 13
Mitglied 63
mitnehmen 50
Mittagessen 45
möchte wissen 27
Modell 13, 26, 30
mögen 47, 50
möglich 42
Mönch 28
Mörder 32, 46
morgen 14, 22
morgen früh 59
morgen vormittag 59
müde 26
Musik 20, 47
Musiker 61
müssen 25

nach oben 38
Nachbar(in) 63
nachdenken 31
Nachfolger 29
nachmittag 22
Nacht 61
Nähe 39
Name 38
national 44
nehmen 46, 56
nennen 38
nett 35
neu 58
neuernannt 44
neueste 30
Nichtfachmann 37
nörgeln 9
normalerweise 46
nötig 25
notwendig 25

oben 24, 38
offenbar 19
offenhalten 61
offenlassen 60
Offizier 35
Öl 56
operieren 28, 59
Opfer 19

Päckchen 43
Paket 2, 43
Partie 48
passieren 60, 61
Patient 28, 57
Patientin 57
Pferd 31
Pflicht 59
Plan 53
Plattform 29
Podium 29
Politiker 10, 19
Polizist 39
Preis 19, 20, 56
Preiserhöhung 9
pro 16
Problem 28, 42, 49, 50
Produkt 18
Projekt 36
pünktlich 22, 26
putzen 28

rasieren 40
Rasierwasser 14
Rat 10
raten 29, 36
Rathaus 12
Ratschlag 8
rauchen 11, 38
Rechnung 12
Rechtsanwalt 11, 25, 42
Rede 57
reden über 18
Regenschirm 28
reichen 30
Reis 18
reisen 26

GRAMMATIKREGISTER

Die Zahlen bezeichnen die Seiten.

DIE ZEICHEN DER LAUTSCHRIFT

[ʌ]	wie in *luck* [lʌk], *gun* [gʌn]
[ɑː]	wie in *last* [lɑːst], *arm* [ɑːm]
[ai]	wie in *ice* [ais], *time* [taim]
[au]	wie in *shout* [ʃaut], *brown* [braun]
[æ]	wie in *black* [blæk], *hand* [hænd]

[e]	wie in *let* [let], *egg* [eg]
[ei]	wie in *make* [meik], *name* [neim]
[ɛə]	wie in *fair* [fɛə], *care* [kɛə]
[ə]	wie in *away* [ə'wei], *colour* ['kʌlə]
[əː]	wie in *first* [fəːst], *burn* [bəːn]
[əu]	wie in *hope* [həup], *home* [həum]

[i]	wie in *sit* [sit], *will* [wil]
[iː]	wie in *eat* [iːt], *clean* [kliːn]
[iə]	wie in *here* [hiə], *clear* [kliə]

[ɔ]	wie in *hot* [hɔt], *wrong* [rɔŋ]
[ɔː]	wie in *water* ['wɔːtə], *fall* [fɔːl]
[ɔi]	wie in *voice* [vɔis], *boy* [bɔi]

[u]	wie in *book* [buk], *full* [ful]
[uː]	wie in *shoot* [ʃuːt], *soon* [suːn]
[uə]	wie in *sure* [ʃuə], *poor* [puə]

[ŋ]	wie in *king* [kiŋ], *song* [sɔŋ]
[s]	wie in *sit* [sit], *kiss* [kis]
[z]	wie in *zoo* [zuː], *crazy* ['kreizi]
[θ]	wie in *thing* [θiŋ], *both* [bəuθ]
[ð]	wie in *then* [ðen], *other* ['ʌðə]
[ʃ]	wie in *shine* [ʃain], *fish* [fiʃ]
[ʒ]	wie in *pleasure* ['pleʒə], *television* ['teliviʒn]
[v]	wie in *visit* ['vizit], *leave* [liːv]

[']	steht vor der betonten Silbe: *after* ['ɑːftə], *about* [ə'baut]

ENGLISCH FÜR SIE
Ein moderner Sprachkurs für Erwachsene

Englisch für Sie 1

Lehrbuch – Hueber-Nr. 2127

4 Schallplatten (Lektionstexte und *Pronunciation Exercises*) –
Hueber-Nr. 2.2127

1 Tonband (inhaltsgleich mit 2.2127) – Hueber-Nr. 7.2127*

2 Tonbänder (Lektionstexte m. Nachsprechpausen) – Hueber-Nr. 8.2127**

3 Compact-Cassetten (inhaltsgleich mit 8.2127) – Hueber-Nr. 9.2127***

1 Compact-Cassette (inhaltsgleich mit 8.2127) – Hueber-Nr. 18.2127*

Arbeitsbuch 1 – Hueber-Nr. 14.2127

Sprechübungen 1:
  Textheft – Hueber-Nr. 13.2127
  6 Tonbänder – Hueber-Nr. 5.2127**
  6 Compact-Cassetten – Hueber-Nr. 17.2127*
  4 Schallplatten (Auswahl aus den Grammatik-Drills) –
    Hueber-Nr. 6.2127

Zusatzprogramm für Sprachlabor- und Klassenunterricht:
  Textheft – Hueber-Nr. 2172
  3 Tonbänder – Hueber-Nr. 2.2172**
  3 Compact-Cassetten – Hueber-Nr. 3.2172*

Diktatkurs 1 (2 Schallplatten mit Textheft) – Hueber-Nr. 16.2127

Lektüren:
  Leichte Lesetexte – Hueber-Nr. 3.2127
  Lektüreheft 1 – Hueber-Nr. 32.2127
  Lektüreheft 2 – Hueber-Nr. 33.2127
  Lektüreheft 3 – Hueber-Nr. 34.2127

Englisch für Sie 2

Lehrbuch – Hueber-Nr. 2128

3 Schallplatten (Lektionstexte) – Hueber-Nr. 2.2128

2 Tonbänder (Lektionstexte mit Nachsprechpausen) –
Hueber-Nr. 8.2128**

1 Compact-Cassette (inhaltsgleich mit 8.2128) – Hueber-Nr. 18.2128*

Arbeitsbuch 2 – Hueber-Nr. 14.2128

Sprechübungen 2:
  Textheft – Hueber-Nr. 13.2128
  5 Tonbänder – Hueber-Nr. 5.2128**
  15 Compact-Cassetten – Hueber-Nr. 17.2128*
  3 Schallplatten (Auswahl aus den Grammatik-Drills) –
    Hueber-Nr. 6.2128

Lektüren:
    Lektüreheft 1 – Hueber-Nr. 32.2128
    Lektüreheft 2 – Hueber-Nr. 33.2128
    Lektüreheft 3 – Hueber-Nr. 34.2128

Englisch für Sie 3

Lehrbuch – Hueber-Nr. 2129
3 Schallplatten (ausgewählte Lektionstexte) – Hueber-Nr. 2.2129
1 Tonband (ausgewählte Lektionstexte mit Nachsprechpausen) –
    Hueber-Nr. 8.2129**
1 Compact-Cassette (inhaltsgleich mit 8.2129) – Hueber-Nr. 18.2129*
Arbeitsbuch 3 – Hueber-Nr. 14.2129
Sprechübungen 3:
Texfheft – Hueber-Nr. 13.2129
7 Tonbänder – Hueber-Nr. 5.2129**
7 Compact-Cassetten   Hueber-Nr. 17.2127*
Lektüren:
    Lektüreheft 1 – Hueber-Nr. 32.2129
    Lektüreheft 2 – Hueber-Nr. 33.2129
    Lektüreheft 3 – Hueber-Nr. 34.2129

ERGÄNZEND ZU DEN BÄNDEN 1–3

Englisch-deutsches Lernwörterbuch – Hueber-Nr. 2144
Englische Wortschatzübungen – Hueber-Nr. 2165
Englische Mindestgrammatik – Hueber-Nr. 2155
Englische Sprachgebrauchsübungen – Hueber-Nr. 2178
Englische Taschengrammatik – Hueber-Nr. 2185

Englisch für Sie · Aufbaukurs Wirtschaft

Lehrbuch – Hueber-Nr. 2167
Schallplattenprogramm Englisch Wirtschaft – Hueber-Nr. 3.2167
Cassettenprogramm Englisch Wirtschaft – Hueber-Nr. 4.2167*
Tonbandprogramm Englisch Wirtschaft – Hueber-Nr. 5.2167**
Englisch-deutsches Lernwörterbuch Wirtschaft – Hueber-Nr. 6.2167
Arbeitstexte Englisch Wirtschaft – Hueber-Nr. 7.2167

---

    * Doppelspuraufnahme, auf allen Cassetten-Recordern bzw. Tonbandgerä-
      ten abspielbar
  ** Halbspuraufnahme mit freier Schülerspur, 9,5 cm/sec, auf allen Tonband-
      geräten und im Sprachlabor einsetzbar
*** Parallelspuraufnahme, abspielbar auf Normalrecordern (keine Aufnahme-
      möglichkeit) und Zweispur-Cassettengeräten (mit Aufnahmemöglichkeit)